THE VERLINDEN WAY VOLUME IV
scale models and dioramas

by François Verlinden

SECOND PRINT MARCH 1986

VERLINDEN PUBLICATIONS

Contents

Nerve Center	3
Korean Wolf	7
American Samurai	11
On the double!	16
The Ignorant D-Day minus one	18
Temporary Residence	22
Brief Encounter	26
Paradise by the Desert side	30
Chariot of Fire	32
Breach to Victory	36
Commander's Delight	39
Heavy Weight Centipede	43
Knocked Out!	49

© Copyright: 1985 by **Verlinden Publications**
a **Verlinden & Stok pvba** division
Berlaarsestraat 36
2500 Lier/Belgium
All rights reserved.
No part of this book may be reproduced, stored in
a retrieval system or transmitted in any form by
any means, electronic, mechanical, photocopying,
recording or otherwise, without written permission
of **Verlinden Publications**.
ISBN 90 70932 04 0

All scale models and photographs by François Verlinden unless otherwise indicated.

Text: Hans Wilms
Artwork and lay-out: Willy Peeters

Nerve Center

For those modelers who love ultimate detail and are charmed by aviation technology and everything it takes to fly an airplane, Esci has taken the initiative to produce large 1/12 scale cockpits of wellknown aircraft. The first kit to be released was the F-16 cockpit, followed by the F-104. The F-16 is reviewed here for the simple reason that the F-104 cockpit was not yet available when this book was set up.

Opening the box is a breathtaking experience. First of all it takes a while to get used to the size of the model. The large bathtub and big parts of the seat and instrument panel is beyond the experience of most modelers. The detail is at first sight overwhelming. You cannot help but being amazed by the molding detail on the panels, switches, seat and so on. However, if you know your bits and pieces of the F-16 and start checking out the detail, you will find various mistakes. But they are not of such a nature that it is close to impossible to correct them. The biggest problem is the headrest of the seat. Even without correcting these faulty details the kit is very impressive when finished.

The model depicts an F-16A block 10 cockpit, but for those who want to make a block 15 cockpit, it is a piece of cake. You just have to change the location of some panels and instruments and make two new ones. Our book 'Lock-on n° 2 The General Dynamics F-16 Fighting Falcon' will prove to be a great help both in completing the kit as is or converting it into a block 15. And if you want to go for the ultimate realism, we produce authentic film-type instruments for this model. Their use is depicted in this chapter.

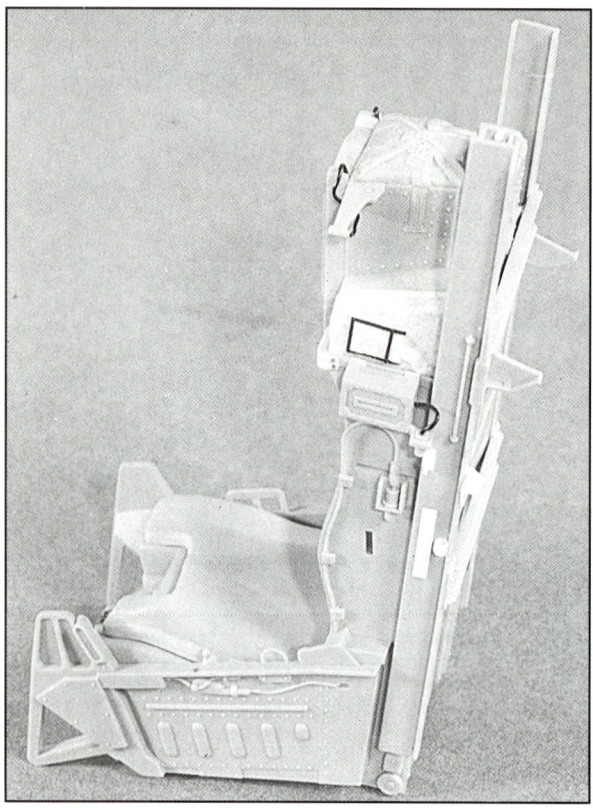
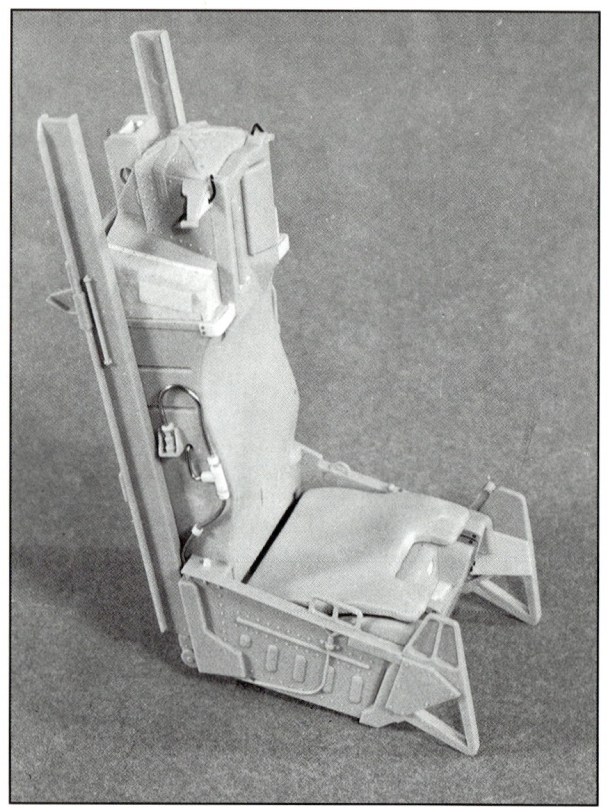

These two pictures illustrate the extra-detailing of the ACES II ejection seat. As said the headrest is not all together correct, but in this case it was left unchanged. The additional detail includes detailed parachute packs and environmental sensors, altered pyrotechnic firing lines and some detail on the seat rails. Changing the headrest involves extensive rebuilding and a lot of scratchbuilt parts which can only be effected with the aid of good pictures.

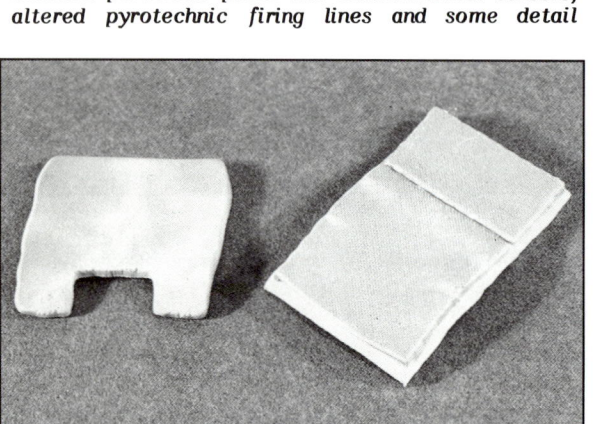

The seat cushions that come with the kit are not very realistic as they are too stiff and neat. It is much better to make new ones from an epoxy putty and some tissue paper.

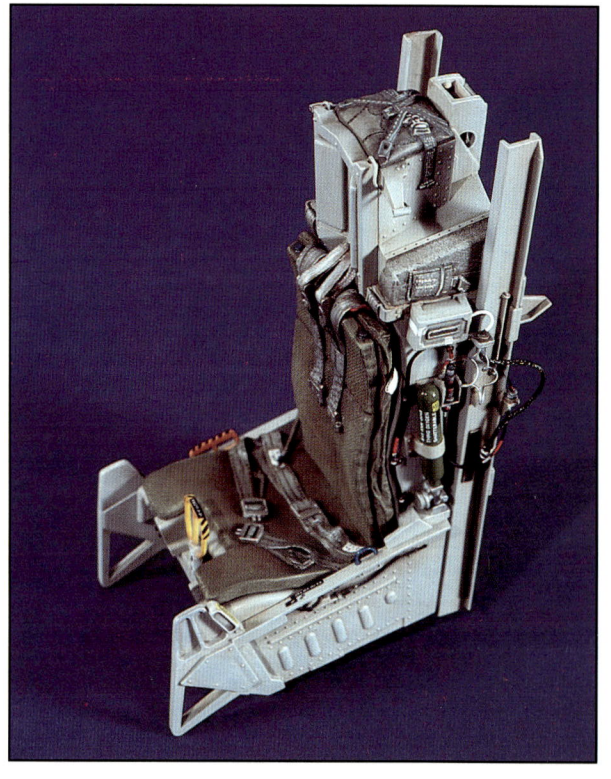

When the seat is painted and weathered the result is close to perfect. It should be noted that the larger the model, the more critical the paintjob becomes. Experience is imperative with large scale models like these.

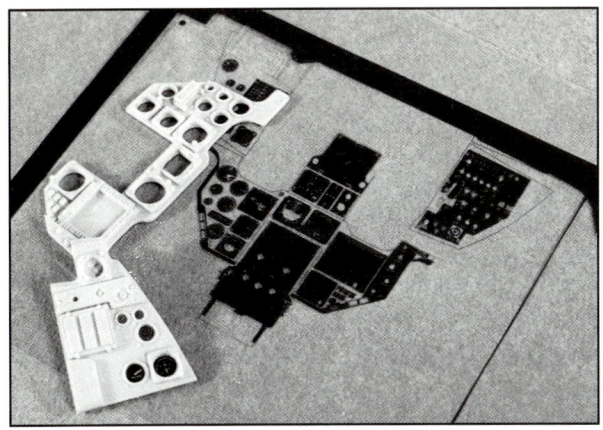

Our film-type instruments have been reproduced from the pilot's manual, thus are authentic. There are a couple of ways in which you can use them. They are all described in the enclosed instructions.

It is hard to tell a real cockpit from this model finished with the instruments shown at left. With a little effort you could add light behind the instruments to make the model even more life-like.

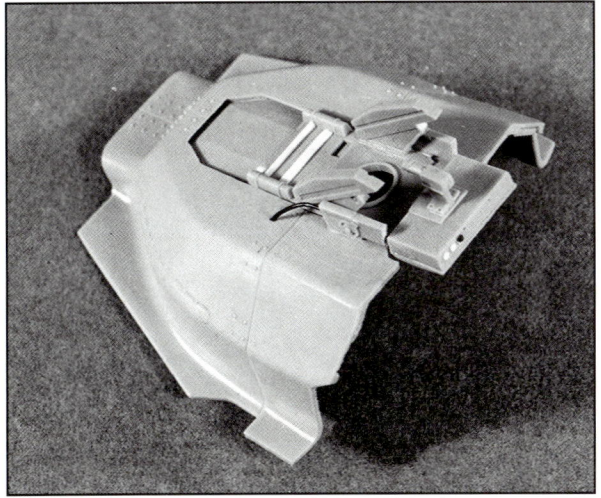

The instrument panel cover needs a little extra-detailing. This is limited to a few pieces of wire and some plastic strip.

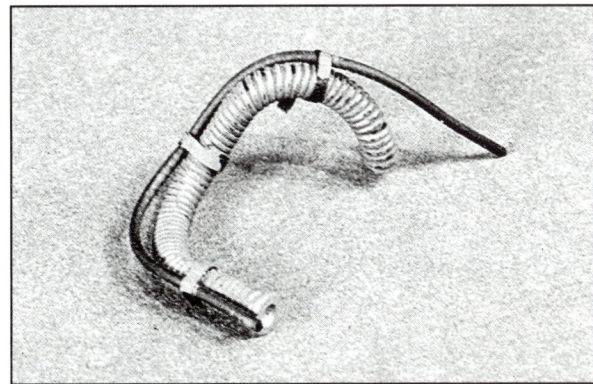

The audio connection, which hooks up to the headset in the pilot's helmet, was made of copper wire and fixed to the oxygen hose with graphic tape.

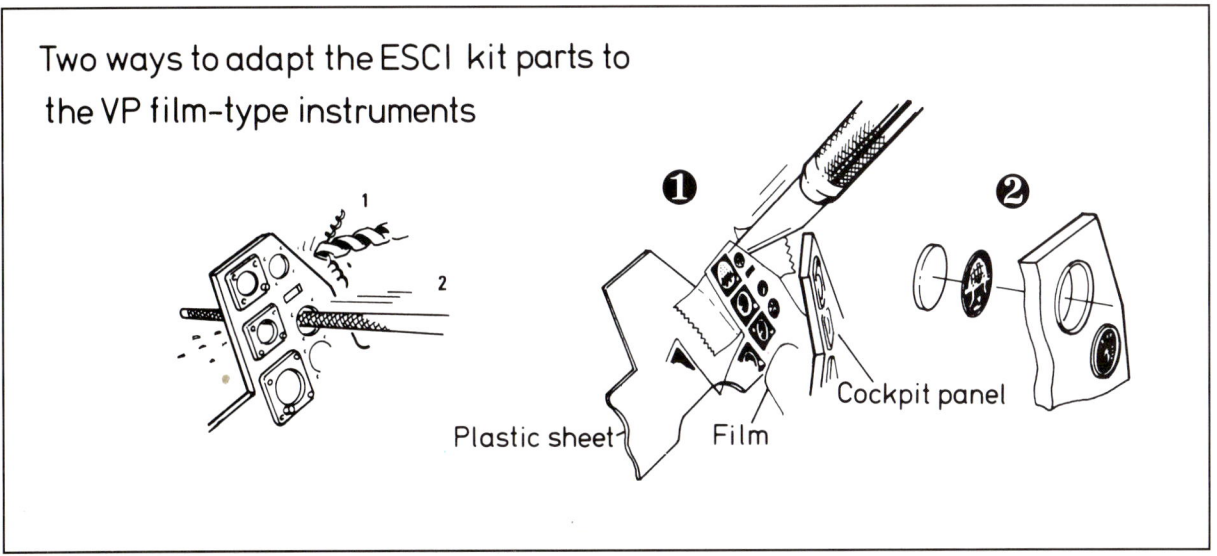

Two ways to adapt the ESCI kit parts to the VP film-type instruments

Korean Wolf

It seems that Hasegawa is one of the few kit manufacturers that realised it was high time to produce what the modeler wants, not what the manufacturer thinks the modeler might need. For many years aircraft modelers have been asking for detailed cockpits and ejection seats, recessed panel lines, a wider variety of weapons and so on. Well, we have got most of it, although some small details are still left to be desired.

In this particular case of the F-16 on 48th scale we miss the typical centerline tank and a seperate tail fairing to make a Norwegian or Belgian F-16. That is to say, those items would make the kit complete. They can however quite easily be scratchbuild, so there is no real problem there.

What we do get, is a beautifully molded model, with near to perfect recessed panel lines, cockpit transparencies of excellent quality, an ACES II seat (finally) as featured in all production F-16's, up-to-date block 15 features like the increased area tail planes and, in combination with Hasegawa's weapon sets, the possibility to arm the F-16 up to its teeth.

There were times when the Hasegawa decals were a true nightmare. This is no longer so. At present they are of first-rate quality and work very well with a decal setting agent. The milky film of yesteryear truly belongs to the past.

Assembling the model does not bring along any surprises except for the fit of the wings to the body. This area needs quite some attention to make the wing-body blend what it should be. It is adviseable to make the upper surfaces match perfectly and sand the body strakes on the underside. Apart from that there are no hang-ups.

You can of course go for as much super-detail as you like, depending on your skills and desires. The next pages will give you some ideas in this direction. The unexperienced modeler may find the illustrated detail jobs way too complicated, the super-modeler may find them to be below standards. But then, it is the large group of average

Finished in the fighting colors of the 35 TFS, 8 TFW 'Wolf Pack' based on Kunsan AB, Korea and loaded with various stores taken from the valuable Hasegawa weapons sets, the model catches the aggresiveness of the F-16 to advantage.

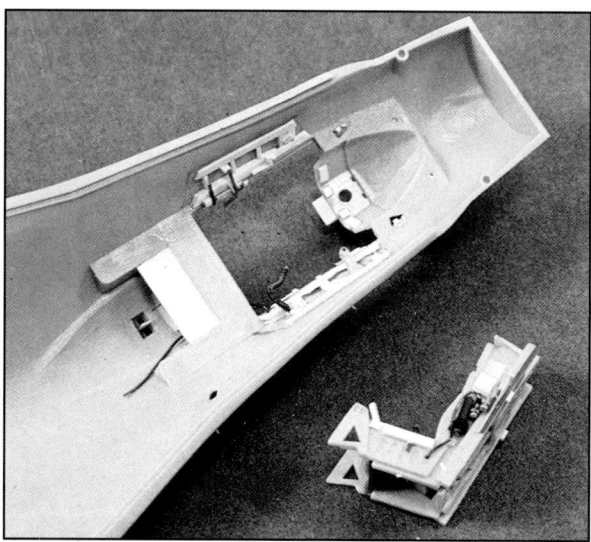

Although this Hasegawa kit is one of the most exact models of the F-16, there is room for improvements. Kit manufacturers have lately been devoting more time to the cockpit interiors, but most kits are still badly in need for much more of it.
In this case the cockpit side walls were built up with plastic strip and rod. And while you are at it you may just as well tackle the underside of the instrument panel cover.

This is what the finished, unpainted cockpit tub and seat look like. Although the aft bulkhead of the tub should be to the vertical, there is no sense in changing it since it can not be seen anyway. Note the ejection seat handle on the seat as well as the position of the utility light and the oxygen hose.

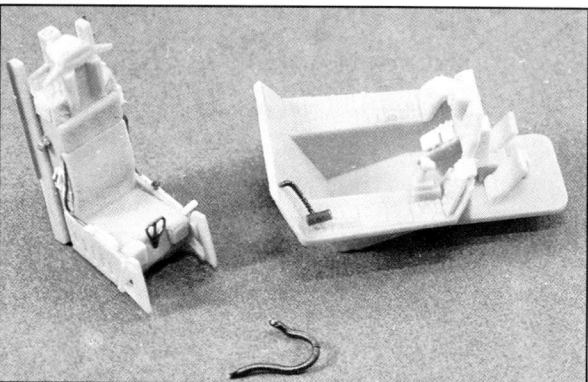

The cockpit tub is fairly accurate as it is, so the only thing that needs to be added is the utility light on the right console. A few pieces of plasticard make up the electro-optical display and the instruments directly above it. Note the additional details on the seat and the oxygen hose.

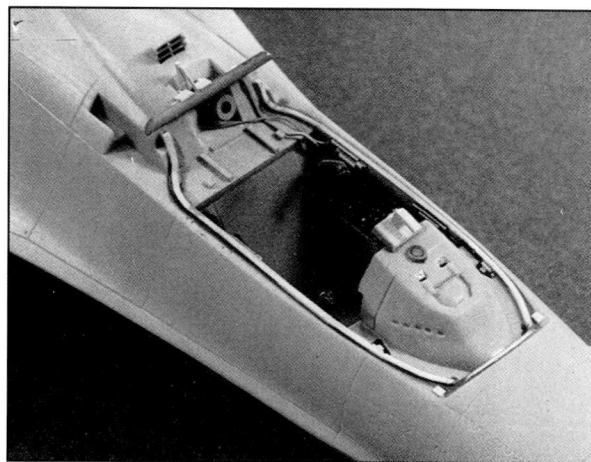

The cockpit tub has been installed and the sill and area aft of the seat have been detailed with pieces of strip and rod and fine copper wire.

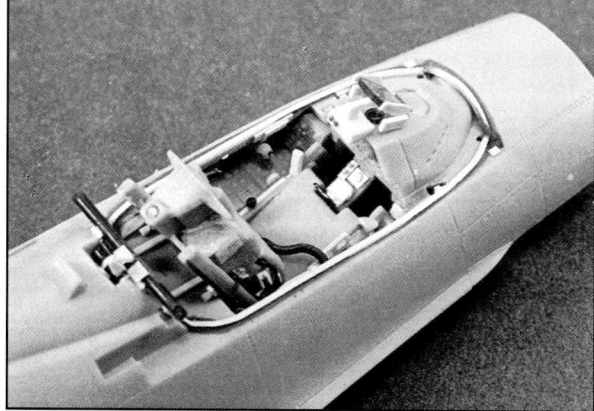

Another view of the cockpit with the seat installed. A video camera has been added under the HUD combiner glass. The mounting frame of the latter and the indexers on both sides of it are simple pieces of plastic strip.

The main gear wells of the F-16 hold most of its auxiliary equipment. Some of it, like the aircraft battery, the halon tank and hydraulic oil filters and tubing, is very prominent and really should be added.

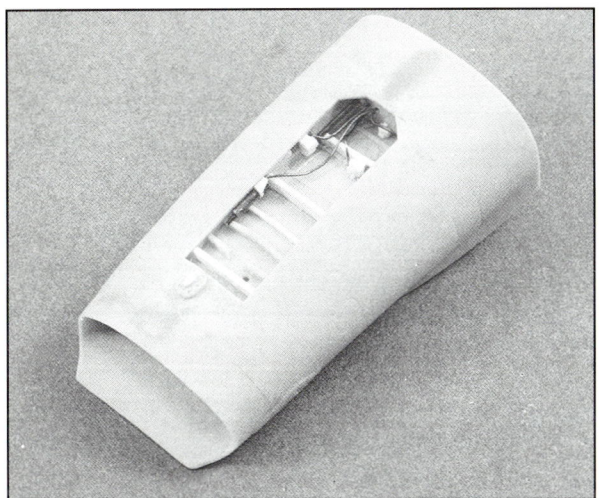

The nose gear well of the F-16 is very simple. It only carries a few sequencers that can be simulated with plasticard. Their connections are made with copper wire.

The finished cockpit with opened hood. Note the safety pin flag on the seat.

Although some of the details in the main gear wells may be oversized they still look very convincing when painted and weathered.

This picture, together with the one on the top left, enable you to detail your model as well. It may look complicated, but in fact it is not. The only things you need is some plastic strip and rod, maybe some parts out of the scrapbox and the courage to sit down and do it.

Here the canopy has been deleted to show the interior of the cockpit of the completely finished model. The molding seam on the canopy transparency can be removed by sanding it off with very fine sanding paper and consequently polishing it with toothpaste and finally car polish.

Another view of the finished model from a different angle. The installation of the AMRAAM's on the stations 2 and 8 is a little premature, although most of the late block 15 aircraft already have part of the hardware for the system. This model is just a little ahead of time.

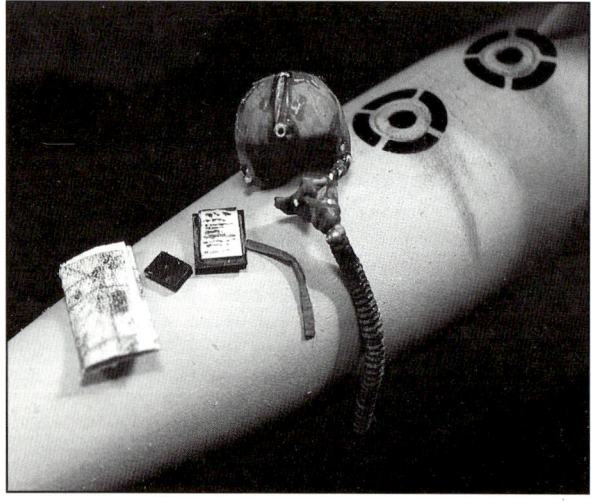

Being a succesful modeler means amongst other things having eye for small details. Here a camouflaged helmet, a kneepad, a video casette and a map have been placed on the port external tank to enhance realism.

modelers in the middle that this book aims at.

The three or four different shades of grey that are used on today's USAF and NATO fighters have been subject to heated debates over and over again. In official papers they are designated as FS 36118 Dark Grey, FS 36270 Medium Grey, FS 36375 Light Compass Grey and FS 36320 Dark Compass Grey, and that is all very nice, but..... Take four different brands of paint and you have four different tones of each grey. And, what's more, many 'experts' will tell anybody who wants to know that none of them is correct. Some will say they are too bluish, other will state they are too grey. Both groups are all together right and wrong!

What is it about this colors? The answer is very simple, but makes matters more complicated at the same time. It was precisely the intention to develop a kind of paint that appears to be of a different shade every time the light conditions change. We have hundreds of photographs of F-16s, not one looks alike. Sunrise, sunset, a bright sunny day or cloudy skies, they all cause a difference in shades. Sometimes the greys seem to be bluish, then again brown-grey, light grey or dark grey. This means you can use any shade you prefer and that's that. Just leave the 'experts' for what they are!

American Samurai

Of all Phantom models in various scales the recently released Hasegawa series on 48th scale is without doubt the best. Finally a manufacturer succeeded in capturing the impressive lines of the F-4 correctly. And when they introduced recessed panel lines starting with the F-4E, the perfect Phantom model was born. Although the cockpit detail is not all together complete, the exterior is correct down to the smallest detail. Next to that Hasegawa have improved their decal quality to such an extent that they can be called first rate. Not only do they work very well, the artwork is also impressive. For that reason I chose to make this Japanese F-4EJ. The diorama is kept simple to enhance the beautiful lines and coloring of the model.

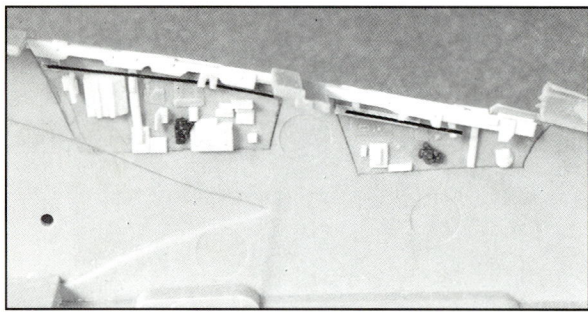

The secret of detailing a model on this scale lies in succesfully simulating detail rather than trying to reproduce it to the last rivet or switch. There is only one way to get to know that secret and that is through trial and error. Experience is the key word here as there is no such thing as a magic recipe.

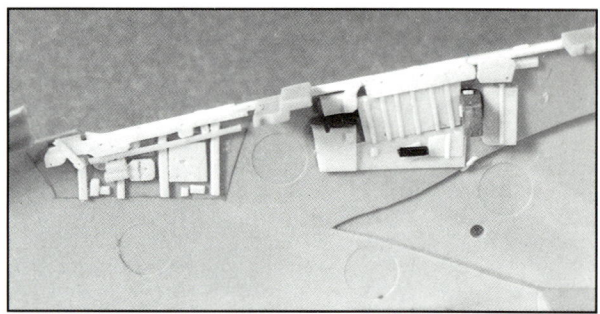

Cockpit detail is excellent apart from the sidewalls that should be crowded with mostly circuit breakers.

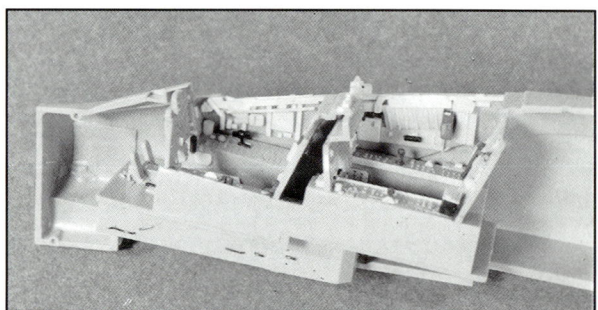

Here the same goes as for the picture on the left.

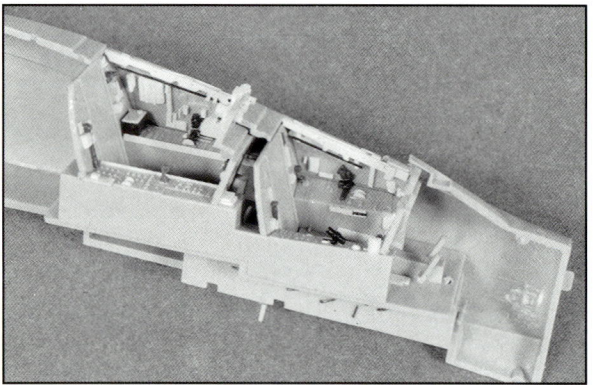

A lot of test fitting is involved to make sure that the added detail does not interfer with the original kit parts. This way you also get a fair idea of what the assembly will look like when completed.

The finished cockpit interior leaves a rather realistic effect. There is no use in going for the ultimate detail on 48th scale. First of all it is not possible, secondly it would be murder on your eyesight. Another part of the cockpit area that needs some detailing is the front of the rear instrument panel. The instruments are not covered and the electric, pneumatic and hydraulic lines are clearly visible, so they need to be added.

An important factor in detailing is the art of painting. Though it does not come easy (you should develop your own style), you should devote a lot of time to it as it really is the finishing touch.

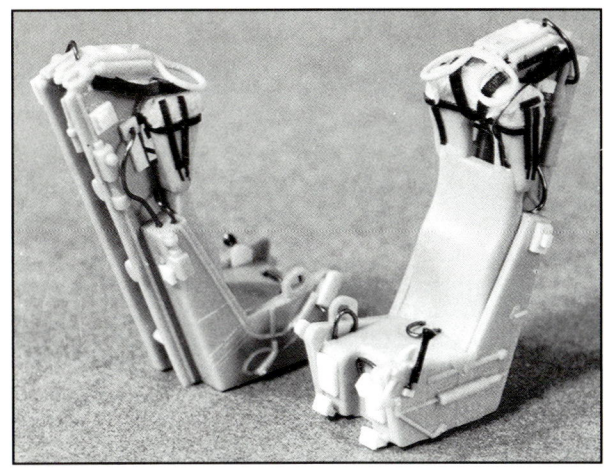

Although the kit's seats are very nice, they still lack detail that the manufacturer simply cannot mold. This mainly concerns wiring, straps, grips, etc. They are quite easy to reproduce with artist's graphic tape, copper wire, plastic rod and so on.

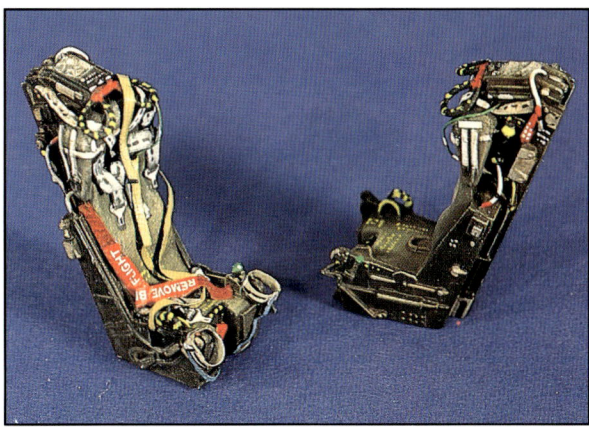

It is the painting that finally brings out the best in a model. The choice of color or rather the shade, is very important and it realy is very difficult to give any leads here. It is mainly a matter of experience and personal taste and that we cannot readily supply.

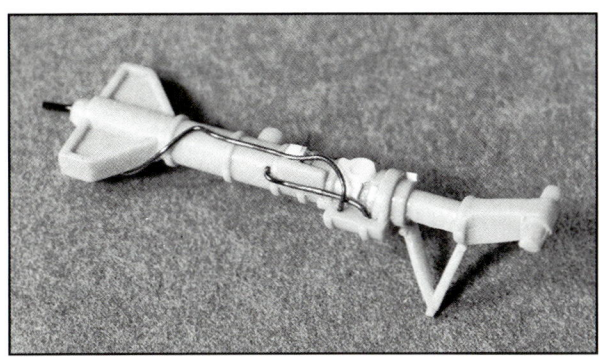

The nose strut lacks hydraulic lines as do the main gear struts. Do not worry too much about exaggerating the dimensions, kit manufacturers do it all the time to enhance the effect. Details exactly to scale sometimes appear to be too small, so be careful.

On most parked F-4E's the gas purge door of the gun is open. This door can easily be made out of a few pieces of thin plasticard.

Most, if not all, canopies in aircraft kits are rather shabby, while in reality they are stuffed with clamps, mirrors, links and so on. Ergo, they should be detailed, especially when they are to be left open. Plastic strip and rod are the materials to use. On this picture the canopies have been masked prior to painting.

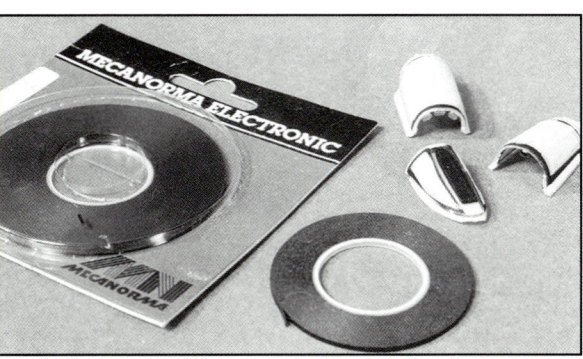

The highly flexible graphic tape used by electronic designers to make masters for printed circuits is ideal for tedious masking jobs, making seat straps, belts and many other uses.

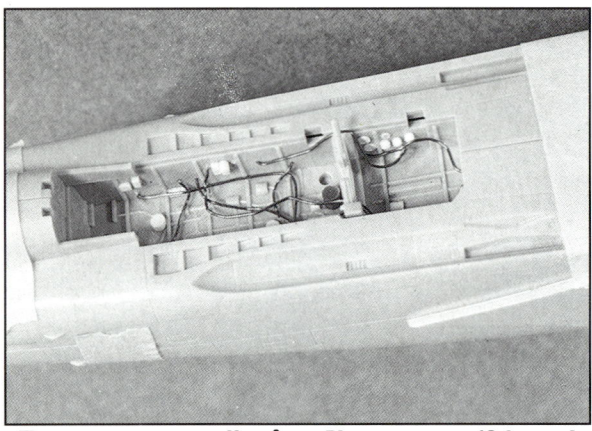

The nose gear well of a Phantom on 48th scale could be accurately detailed, that is if you insist on wasting your eyesight. That does not mean you should do it at random, there should be some authenticity. However, it is better to confine yourself to the most prominent details and simulate these as good as you can.

What looks rather poor on the left picture, turns out to be rather detailed when painted. Of course the gear strut and retraction cylinder take up a lot of the empty space in the well, but good weathering, in this case shading, of the interior is a major part of detailing.

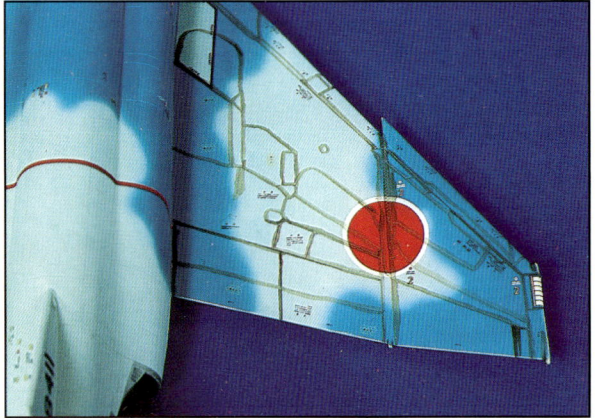

The recessed panel lines should be accented with a wash, i.e. diluted oil paint, to make them stand out more. The wash is run through the panel lines with a fine pointed brush. Before the excess paint is removed, it should be left to settle for a few minutes.

The excess oil paint has been removed with a soft cloth, damp with turpentine. All excess paint should be removed without taking too much of the paint in the lines along.

The details on the upper part of the cockpit still have to be painted. I prefer to do it when the rest is finished. Other people do it first and fix the transparencies before airbrushing the model. The sequence does not realy matter, it is the result that counts.

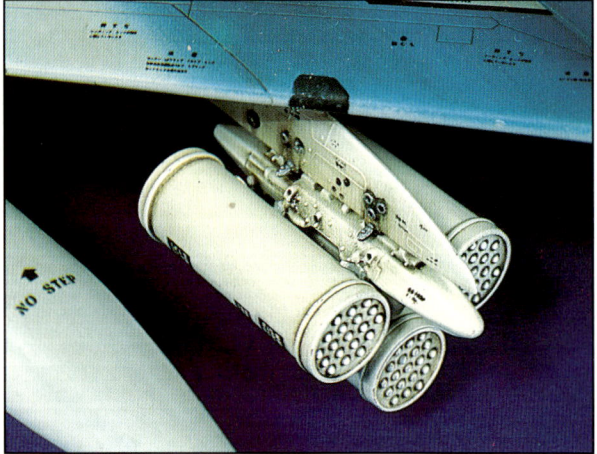

A completely finished weapons pylon in detail. The TER and rocket pods come from Hasegawa's weapon sets, one of the best ideas of the 80's. The subtile weathering brings out the detail on these nicely molded parts.

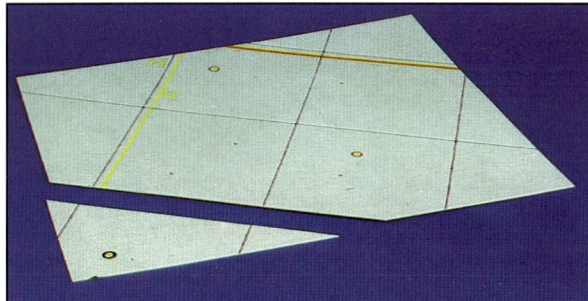

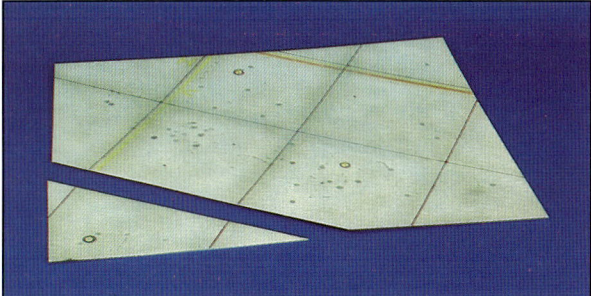

The best way to simulate concrete on dioramas with medium scale models is to use carton. When painted and weathered the appearance is fairly realistic and it is easy to work with.

Small accessories, not available in kit form, have to be scratchbuild. This is not as tough as many people think, provided you have a well-stocked scrapbox. A leftover gas bottle, spare wheels, copper wire and plastic strip make up this home made fire extinguisher.

The ordnance loading tractor in this scene is from Esci's ground equipment set. Finding acceptable figures for a 48th scale diorama is often a problem. Many Monogram kits come with beautiful crew members but the variety of poses is rather limited.

On the double !

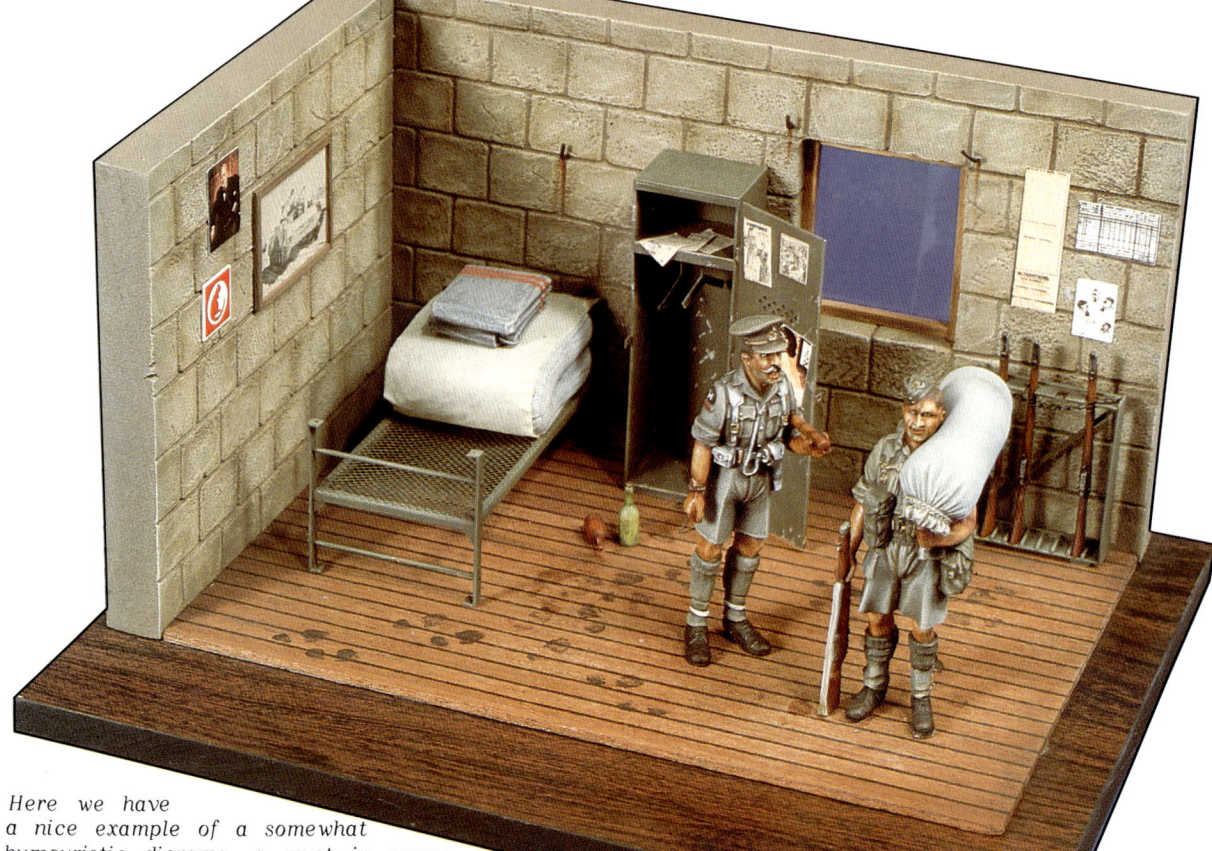

Here we have a nice example of a somewhat humouristic diorama, a must in every collection. They give you a great joy in making.

The scene shows us the barracks of the 8th Army 'Desert Rats' in North Africa. The private obviously spent the night before in the local bar and ruined the tidy room with his muddy feet (not so unlikely in the desert), when coming back with a dissy head and upset stomach. You can still see the hangover on his face. It is also obvious from his messy uniform. Of course the sergeant-major is not pleased with this unsoldier-like appearance and gives the poor man the works. The private is all packed up for some healthy excersise in the open air under the watchful eyes of his superior.

Both the superbly sculpted figures are from the British company Chota Sahib. They are refined into the smallest detail, very well proportioned and the expression on their faces is strikingly real. Painting beautiful figures like these is a real joy and offers a good chance to recuperate from that never-ending converting of plastic figures while still keeping up the skill.

Being soft metal figures they need some special attention in preparing them for painting. First of all the seams have to be carefully filed and sanded. Next the entire figure should be polished extensively with steelwool to remove the oxydes. Take care not to touch food with these oxydes on your hands; they are far from healthy. Wash up first. The next step is to clean the figure with thinner. Then it should be painted with a special metal primer to provide a good bite for the enamels. For the cloths I used Humbrol uniform colors (refer to: 'Monty's 8th Army in the desert', an Osprey publication). The bare skin is painted with artist's oil paints.

The bed, locker and riflerack were all made from plastic sheet, strip and rod. The wire mesh on the bed is simple mosquito netting. The mattrass was formed from epoxy putty. The mattrass cover and blankets are all tissue paper.

The walls were sculpted from 1cm thick balsa planking. The window frame is balsa strip, the pane itself is clear plastic sheet. The picture frame of the 8th Army Crusader photo is also balsa. The picture itself was taken from an old magazine as was the pin-up on the inside of the locker door. The empty bottles are Historex spares.

The floor was made from deck planking as it is used in shipmodeling, the muddy footprints were realised through dipping an old figure's feet in dark brown oil paint and pressing them on the floor. Finally the Lee Enfields in the rack come from the 8th Army Multipose from Airfix.

The bed with mattress and blankets and the empty locker. Note the bottles, pin-up on the inside of the locker door and muddy footprints on the floor.

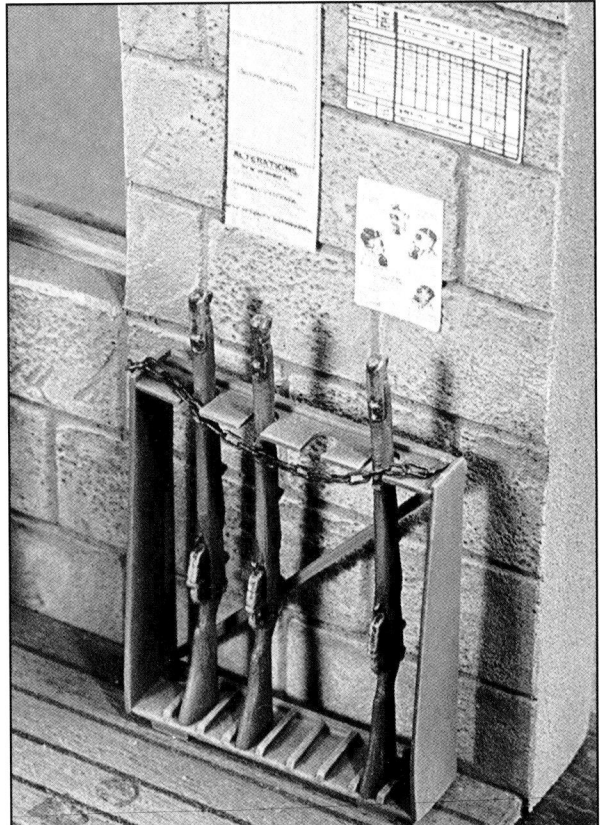

The riflerack made up of plastic sheet. Worth noting are the security chain, the gasmask instruction sheet and planning boards on the wall.

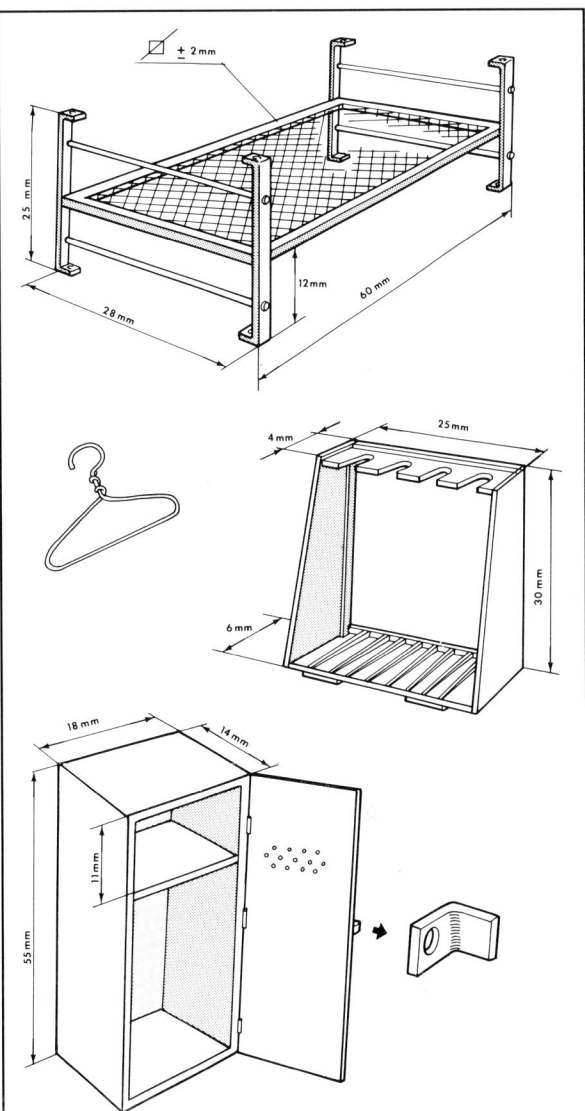

A closer look at the left side wall shows the pictures of Churchill, a Crusader tank and the 'Desert Rats' badge.

The Ignorant   D-Day minus one

The 'Tobruk' pit, as the name denotes, was first employed as an independent emplacement in North Africa. It was a very simple structure comprising an entrance corridor to the left or the right of the actual pit. The pit itself could easily be converted during construction to take a tank turret, shielded anti-tank gun or a machine-gun on a ring, or it could be left empty and used as an observation post. In the Atlantic Wall the 'Tobruk' pit was an integral part of the forward defences. You could even see them incorporated into the roof of a heavy artillery bunker. When constructed as a seperate unit, the emplacements were linked with concrete trenches, some of which were partially covered. They were mostly located on elevated spots like dune tops or even embedded in moles, as can still be seen on Guernsey. When circumstances allowed, the bunkers were concealed by digging them in or banking earth against the sides. In other cases camouflage nets were used.

This diorama is kept rather simple by using the MDA 'Tobruk Pit' and the Tamiya figure set 'German soldiers at rest'. Yet the composition of the scene and the finishing touch added with VP products, like the camouflage nets, barbed wire and signs, make it very attractive.

The MDA kits consists of two parts, an integrated base and sides and the roof. They are nicely molded. Even the planking of the casting molds is simulated. Provided you remove the casting flash and sand the top of the sides and underside of the roof, you should have no problems in mating them up. They can be fixed with any good epoxy cement or contact glue. Some filling of the seam may be necessary. You should try to match the texture of the concrete. The assembly is painted in different shades of khaki drill, starting with the darker one. Remember that concrete is not realy grey, but more a sort of beige, especially when it has been exposed to the natural elements for some time.

The build-up of the scene is pretty basical and clearly illustrated by the pictures on the next few pages. The Tamiya figures were slightly converted to suite the required poses, nothing elaborate and simple to execute. Other items of interest are the hand-made epoxy putty sandbags, the barbed wire and the scattered equipment.

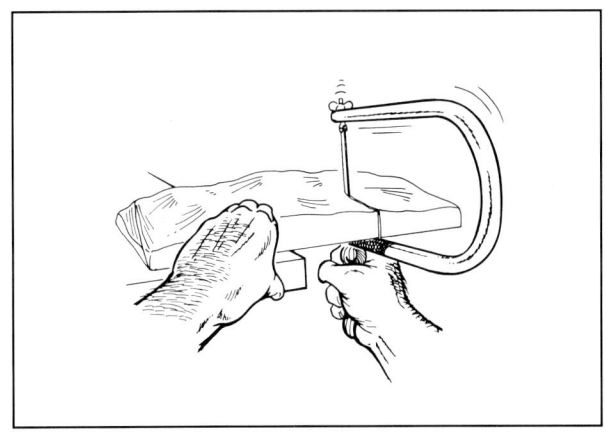

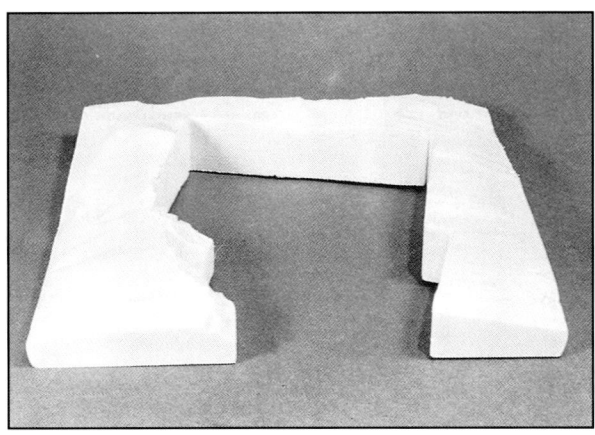

The styrofoam that serves as base for the terrain groundwork has been cut with a fine jigsaw. There are also special styrofoam cutters available that work with a heated wire.

The finished MDA pit. You should keep in mind that concrete is not grey but light beige (advised base color: Humbrol Khaki Drill HM8). Note the interaction between the light and shaded areas. The vegetation on the roof is static grass sprinkled on the still wet dark brown base paint.

The MDA kit and styrofoam have been fixed to the baseplate with contact glue. The edges of the baseplate have been masked with tape to keep them clean during further procedures.

The slightly converted figures from the Tamiya set. By exchanging arms and using heads from the VP metal figure set of heads, the desired pose was accomplished.

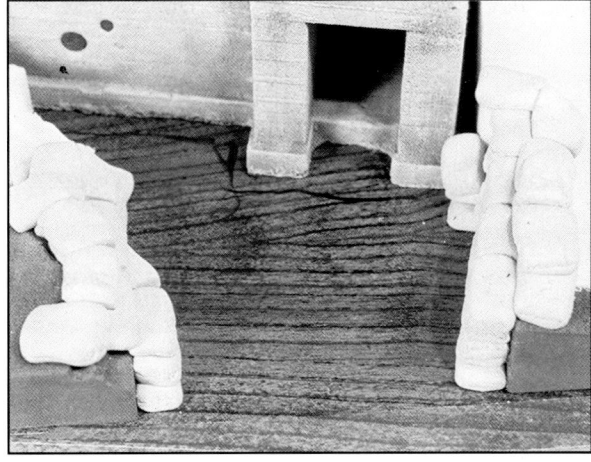

The sandbags are used as protection of the entrances and keep the flanks from eroding in a shower.

The diorama is half-way down the road towards completition. The sides of the styrofoam were painted with waterbase paint, the sandbags have been added. Now the gaps have to be filled with Porion or another scenic plaster.

The guard preparing his lunch is ready to be painted. Before doing so, the figure is pressed lightly into the still soft sandbags to achieve a natural sit.

The sandbags have been painted with Dark Earth as base color and drybrushed with Khaki Drill. Next the static grass was sprinkled in a fair amount in the wet waterbase earth color paint applied to the styrofoam.

The various stages of finishing the groundwork are illustrated here. From left to right you see the bare Porion, base paint and static grass.

The guard on the roof is cutting a loaf. The ever-present German 'Wurst' and ready-to-use weapons are well-illustrated.

A series of detail pictures of the finished diorama. Note the effective use of the VP barbed wire, warning sign from the road sign set and camouflage netting. Also note the scattered weapons.

A little scene at the entrance. A not so well educated soldier offers his bunkie, who has not yet finished his soup, a fag. Again note the personal equipment scattered all over the place and the treaded grass.

A topview of the entire scene. The VP camouflage nets have been fixed to the bunker with invisible matt waterbase varnish. In the topt right corner you can make out a coil of barbed wire and some poles that still have to be placed.

Temporary Residence

This very attractive scene could be laid anywhere from Russia to Normandy. A German infantry squad made an empty 'house' a home. The cellar belongs to a townhouse. The common soldier was and is a true artist in putting to good use all furniture and food left behind by refugees. Some mattresses, some old chairs and a stove are all they need to turn any kind of room into a cosy abode. Anyone who has been with an army fighting unit knows that 'organizing' supplies soon becomes a second nature.

This boxed diorama is in effect very cheap. The only expenses consist of a 'German soldiers at rest' set and a 'German infantry weapons' set, both from Tamiya and a stove from Galia metal castings. All other material that has been used, like the stryrofoam for the walls, the epoxy putty for the mattresses and a supply of plastic sheet and rod, should be readily at hand for all serious modelers. Some of the small items were taken from the scrapbox. True, the material for the shadowbox adds to the budget, but you do not have to go for it, although you can obtain beautiful lighting effects. Day or night, winter or summer, rain or shine, you can simulate it all by varying the position, color and intensity of the lights.

The material needed for the lighting is limited to a transformer, some bulbs with sockets and a main switch plus some wire. Instead of using high voltage mains supply, you could use batteries, which is safer when you do not trust yourself with electricity.

The size of the box is not really important as long as there is enough room to fit the electrical equipment.

The position of the viewing rectangle in the frontal frame is however very important. It draws the viewer's attention to a pre-determined part of the scene that you think to be of prime interest. So take care when cutting the frame, it may be wise to experiment with cardboard templates.

The next pages offer so a sequential review of several stages of completion of this diorama that was a great joy to construct.

The finished styrofoam walls are ready to be fixed to the baseplate. Note that the stairs are only made as far as they are visible.

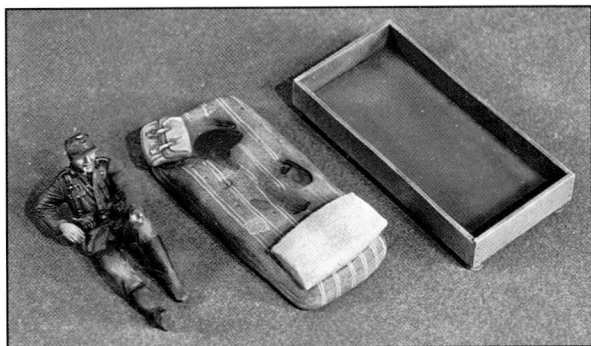

The simple bed made from plastic sheet and strip. The mattress is from epoxy putty. The figure should be pressed lightly into the still soft putty to obtain a natural sit.

The soldiers have picked up a homeless dog that has chosen one of the best spots. The realistically painted mattress is full of fixed tears and patches.

A soldier prepares his meal by slicing bread. The fried egg in the pan simply is a spot of white paint with a yellow dot in the middle to represent the yolk.

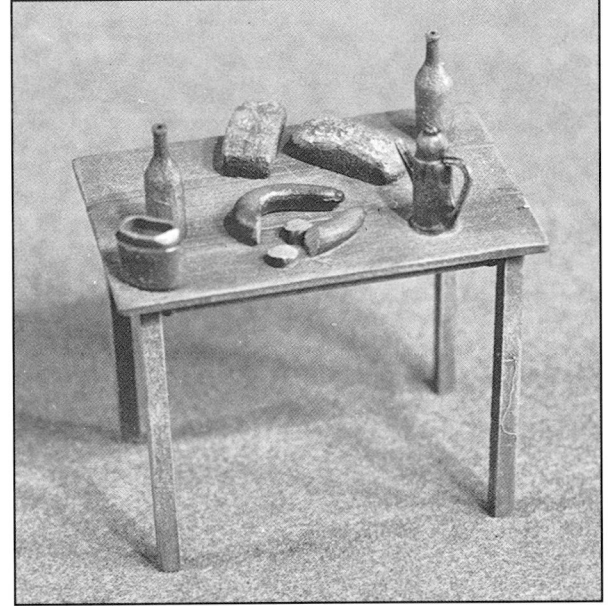

The typical soldier's meal: regular issue loaves, a 'wurst', some 'Ersatz' coffee and the everpresent wine.

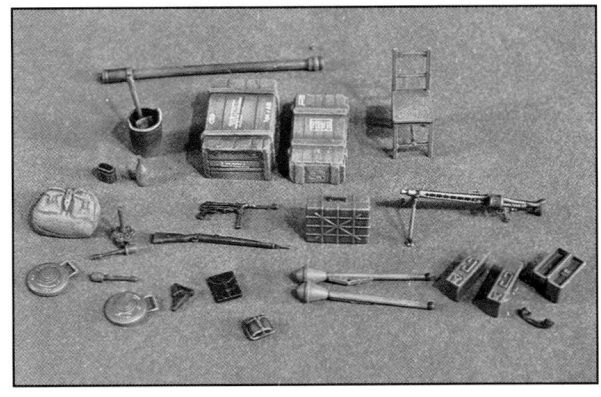

The complete selection of military equipment and small accessories. It takes quite some time to paint all the guns, grenades, mines, crates and so on.

Wiring diagram

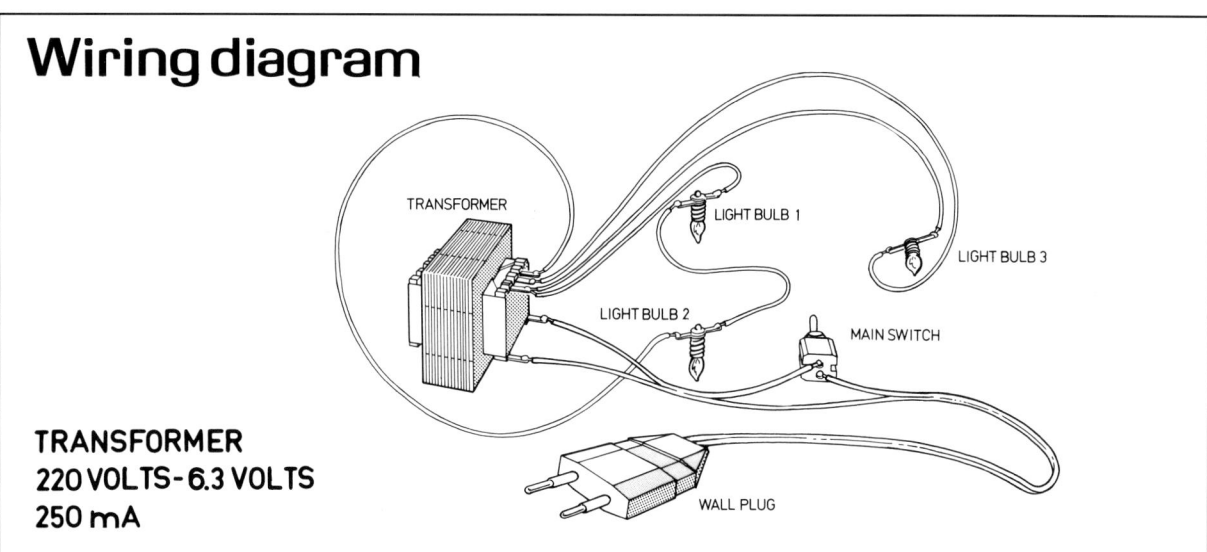

TRANSFORMER
220 VOLTS - 6.3 VOLTS
250 mA

The diorama is fixed to a seperate baseplate that can be removed from the box as a whole. The position of the various light bulbs was determined by trial. Note that there is one at the end of the stairs and one over the venthole.

The ceiling is a simple piece of styrofoam. The wiring is fixed with tape, so it can be removed easily.

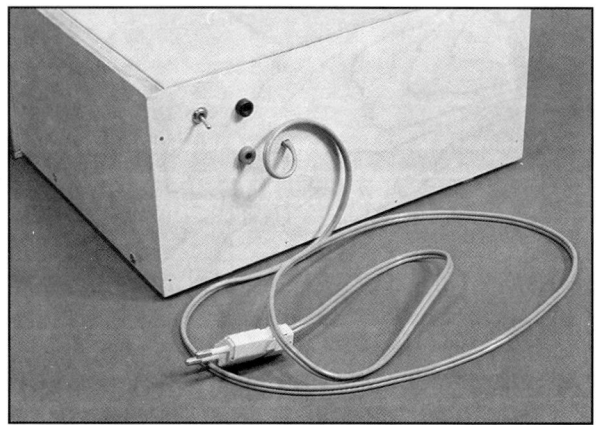

The main power switch is on the back of the box. Further lighting equipment includes a transformer, some bulbs and wire. The latter should be heavy enough to take the current load.

In this case positioning the viewing rectangle was quite easy: right in the middle. In other cases it may take some experimenting before you get it where it is most functional.

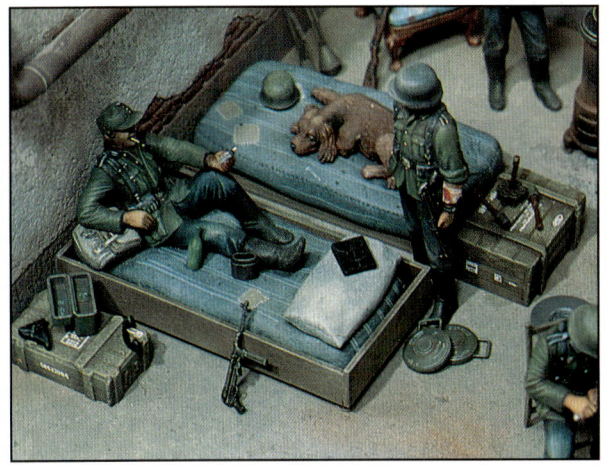

Part of the scene involves two bunkmates having a relaxed smoke. Note the bandage around the arm of the standing soldier.

These two seem to be very pleased with their meal, although I hate to think what might be in that mess-tin.

On this picture you should note the life-like details as there are the sockets on the wall, the iron gate with the coal-scuttle behind it and the weapons and equipment scattered all over.

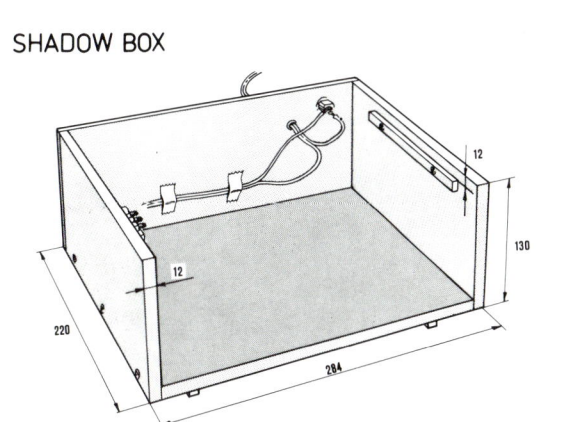

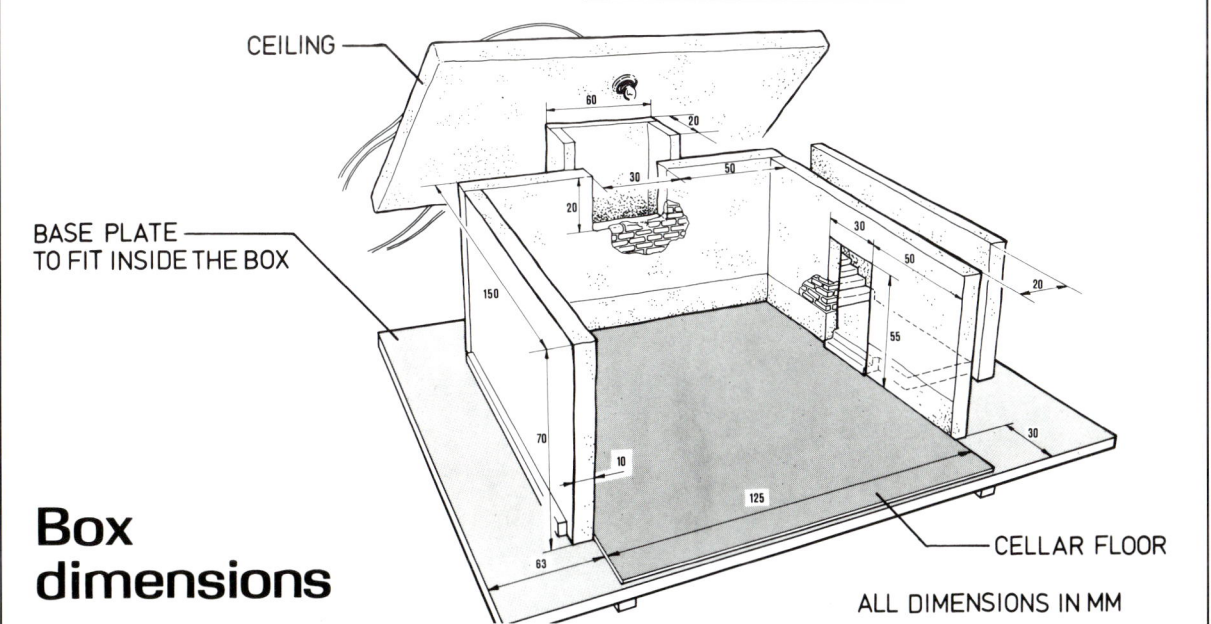

Box dimensions

Brief Encounter

Design of the M1 started as early as 1971, just three months after the ill-fated MBT-70/M803 program was killed by Congress. Because the latter effort had consumed a quarter of a billion dollars without any result, Congress stipulated that the new vehicle was to be kept as simple as possible and intended to keep a very close watch over the cost development. Unit cost was not to exceed half a million 1972 dollars.

The Army decided to go for competitive prototype development which would save a considerable amount of money and time. In 1976 General Motors and Chrysler entered prototypes for trial. Both makes were quite succesful but the Chrysler design was favoured because of the turbine engine. It is smaller, lighter, more powerful and less noisy. The only disadvantage is the higher fuel consumption but the smaller dimensions allow for larger fuel tanks. Moreover the engine is easy to maintain, does not need to be overhauled as frequently as a diesel and has interesting transmission advantages.

The engineering and operational tests revealed initial engine-air filter interface problems which caused turbine blade damage. Congress was immediately on its rear feet and it took Army officials quite some time to convince it that these problems would be sorted out and they were.

The main innovation of the Abrams is the composite armor. Its exact composition is highly classified but it is basically a combination of layers of rolled steel armor plates and ceramics. The latter deflect the heat of shaped-charge anti-tank rounds. Tests with all known Soviet anti-armor ammunitions showed that non can penetrate the frontal armor. The rear portion of the chassis was penetrated but the compartmentalized lay-out of the tank prevented any severe mechanical damage. After track repair the vehicle could be started up and driven away. Further protection is assured by the fully isolated fuel cells and ammunition racks. The ready rounds are stowed behind sliding doors in the turret bustle. In case of a detonation the blast is channeled upward through panels in the turret roof instead of forward into the fighting compartment. Needless to say that the electronic gun-laying equipment enables fire-on-the-move, night fighting and long-range accuracy. The US Army has ordered 7,000 M1s at a drive-away unit cost of $ 1.84 million.

The Tamiya model is fairly accurate. Just the external fire extinguisher actuator on the left sponson and some additional plates on the gun mantlet have to be added. Recently the track skirt plates protecting the drive sprockets have been modified by cutting out a section, because of initial problems in muddy terrain. I chose to delete them all together as was often the case before the modification was carried out. Apart from these minor modifications the model is very easy and fast to build. I have added a gun blast simulator on the barrel, taken from the Italeri Leopard A4 kit.

The pyrotechnic gunfire simulator from the Italeri Leopard A4 fixed to the bore evacuator of the M1 barrel. The clamp needed some adjustment to fit exactly. The electric wiring running along the barrel into the loader's hatch still has to be added.

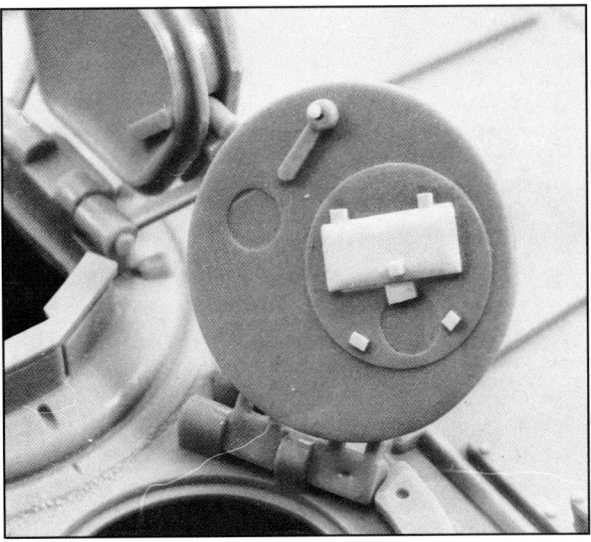

One of the deficiencies of this kit, as on most other kits for that matter, is the lack of inside detail on the hatch covers. It is rather easy to overcome, but each time it is quite an attempt on your scrapbox. I would rather see the manufacturer take care of it. Here a left-over periscope cover has been used, together with some strip and rod.

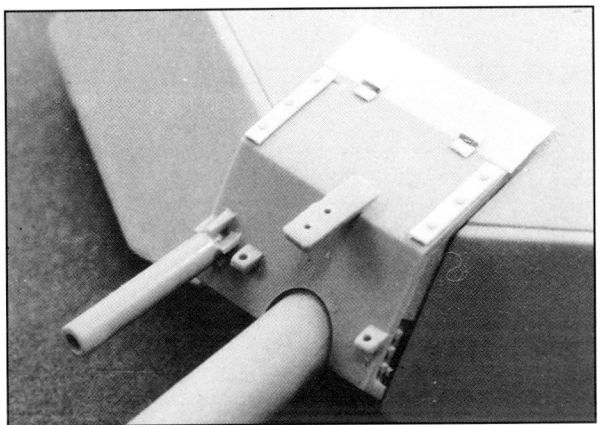

The kit's gun mantlet is not all together complete. A hinged plate has to be added to the rear, while strips with bolts should be glued on the edges.

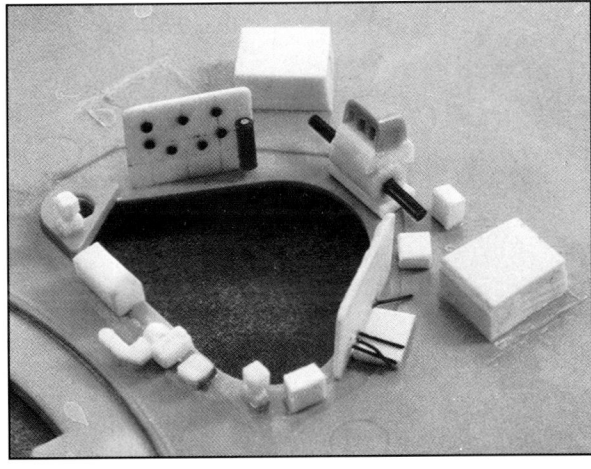

The most important instruments are grouped around the driver's hatch. There is no need to reproduce them faithfully, although you are free to do so if you wish. I simulated them with pieces of plastic strip and rod to at least have something in there in case somebody takes a closer look.

The driver's compartment was built up with random pieces of plasticard, taking care that the hull top would still fit. The instrument consoles are mostly random detail. There are not too many good pictures of the M1 interior and especially the driver's compartment comes in second, so most of the detail is good guesswork.

The model is finished in the four-color MERDC pattern, as most US Army vehicles are at present. Recently however newly delivered vehicles are painted in pre-MERDC Forest Green. This also seems to be a temporary matter, untill someone finally decides what the standard camouflage will be. The MERDC pattern is quite attractive, but it is tough to weather a model so painted. You run the risk to tone down the light colors too much, so extreme care should be taken.

This picture of the right rear quarter illustrates the uncomplicated rear hull deck. The blast panels on top of the ammo compartments mentioned in the introduction, are clearly visible. The personal equipment has not yet been added in order to show the effect of the weathering.

Photographing dioramas with a suitable background is quite a challenge. To start, you do not really need fancy equipment.

Powdered pastel chalks are a major asset to the good modeler. They allow you to obtain effects that cannot be simulated in any other way, as is witnessed by the stained exhaust grill. Dust deposits are another example of the use of pastels. The antennas on military vehicles are usually bent and tied to clear low bridges, power lines and such, but most of all to make the vehicle's presence less obvious. Stretched sprue antennas on models are best tied with thin nylon fishing line.

Military vehicles on excersise are always packed with personal equipment of the crew. Crates and ration boxes are readily available from hobby shops, bedrolls and tarps are best home-made of tissue paper. The fastening straps are all made of the graphic tape mentioned earlier.

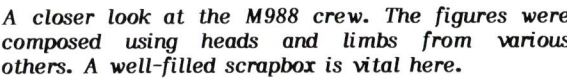

A closer look at the M988 crew. The figures were composed using heads and limbs from various others. A well-filled scrapbox is vital here.

The Sgt. York model has been dealt with elsewhere in this book. This picture illustrates the plain 'Forest Green' camouflage.

Paradise by the Desert side

Due to the ever-growing air-to-ground capacity of the Warsaw Pact air forces it became obvious that the US terrestrial forces are badly in need of something better than the stop-gap M163A1 Vulcan as self-propelled air defence against low level attacks. This sort of weapon system has long been neglected by the US because they never met with serious air-to-ground opposition in Vietnam.

The M163A1 is very limited in performance and the scores in combat are not very overwhelming. The kill-probability against slow non-manoevring aircraft is about thirteen per cent. The track-only radar and simple lead computing sight make the system useless in bad weather, thus useless in Europe and the Old World is still to be considered as the area where IT, if ever, is going to happen. The M163 is however a formidable weapon against ground targets.

In 1977 the US Army requested proposals for an SP Air Defence System with all-weather capability. Ford Aerospace and General Dynamics submitted prototypes. After extensive testing in 1980 the model of the first company was selected.

The twin Bofors 40mm L/70 turret is placed on an M48 hull. The search-while-track radar is derived from the Westinghouse APG-66 used in the F-16. There is an electro-optical backup sight and the vehicles carries 698 rounds in armored bins astride the guns which are completely isolated from the crew compartment. The US Army has ordered 618 M988 Sgt. Yorks to replace the M163 in all regular units.

The Tamiya model was released a little prematurely as is evidenced by the lack of small details on the turret. These can however easily be added using the available pictures in various books as a guide.

Because delivery to the units only started very recently, there is no information available on registration. Therefor I decided to make one of the pilot models on trial in the Californian desert. The M151 TOW, also by Tamiya, was chosen as secondary model.

It is not always that you succeed in making a diorama that is altogether pleasing. Most of the time there are some details that you are not really satisfied with but do not bother to correct because you have to carry on. This is however one of those few dioramas where everything worked out right from the start. The vehicles came out very nice, the figures are very realistic and the various parts of the scenery form a perfect setting.

This overall view of the succeeded diorama offers a good impression of the 'action'. The Sgt. York is passing a publicity poster as they can be found in the US, where the crew of the M151 TOW takes a short break. The poster was cut from a travel agency brochure. The specific logos were hand-painted. The asphalt road came out very well. Note the track marks in the soft surface, molten by the burning sun. Everybody that ever drove through the desert knows that this is what it looks like.

Seldomly a picture of a model comes out as close to perfect as this one. Only a second, much closer look will tell the ignorant viewer that this is not the actual 60 tons of armor steel rolling into your left eye.

A fine study of the right rear quarter of the finished model. Of particular interest is the very nice weathering job and the equipment stowage.

Not only did the Sgt. York come out very well, the USMC M151 TOW worked out fine as well. It is a great secondary model for many a diorama.

Chariot of Fire

The Israeli 'Peace for Galilee' operation in 1982 saw the first massive deployment of the new Merkava MBT. The fact that Israel has to rely on foreign sources for modern heavy military equipment is not exactly to the delight of the political and military leaders of the country. The supply is constantly subject to the mood of the political leaders of the source countries. If it were entirely in the hands of the Israelis they would rather see that their country would be totally self-supporting. Although this is quite impossible, their national industries are manufacturing excellent arms, combat vehicles, aircraft and ammunitions. They have gathered a great deal of experience by modifying existing equipment in the past. Who is not familiar with the improved Shermans, SP artillery on Sherman chassis, almost completely modified Centurion and the Kfir C2, that originates from the French Mirage V. With this experience, the army ordnance depot together with various sub-contractors has developed and built the Merkava, while Israeli Aircraft Industries is developing the Lavi, a fighter that will match the F-16 in performance. Many components of foreign weapon systems used by the Israelis are license manufactured.

The Merkava was not only developed to ensure the constant availability of a modern MBT, but also because the foreign equipment never realy suited the requirments. Only the M-60A3 came close to what the tankers needed.

The prime concern of the designers was the survivability of the crew. Tanks can be produced fairly fast, but to train a crew to a high level of skill takes time and that the Israelis do not have. Therefor optimal protection of the people aboard the vehicle was design goal n° 1, all other specifications being second to that. There you have the reason for the engine being up front, the large escape hatch in the rear of the hull, the elaborate spaced armor, seperate fuel tanks and perfectly sloping armor.

The comfort is quite remarkable for a combat vehicle. The fighting compartment is quite spacious, an airconditioner keeps temperatures down at an acceptable level and a cooled fresh water tank is provided to take care of thirsty throats. The cross-country ride is said to be very smooth.

The only drawback compared to other western tanks is the somewhat inferior top speed. This does not seem to be too much of a problem, as most of the fighting in the Middle East is done under very difficult off-road conditions that do not allow for high speeds. To deal with this minor problem the designers are contemplating on replacing the under-powered Continental diesel by a turbine engine similar to the one used in the M-1 Abrams. This can make the Merkava one of the top three tanks in the world next to the M-1 and Leopard II.

The completed diorama with the MDA Middle East Ruin as setting for the impressive Merkava model. A simple and yet attractive scene with a story of it's own to tell.

Two pictures of the completely finished model. The load of personal equipment in the turret basket is typical for Israeli vehicles.

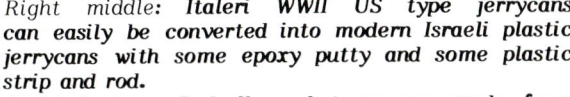

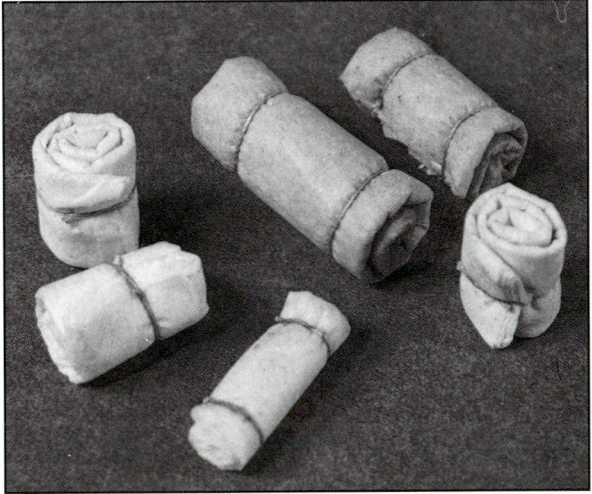

Right middle: Italeri WWII US type jerrycans can easily be converted into modern Israeli plastic jerrycans with some epoxy putty and some plastic strip and rod.

Right bottom: Bedrolls and tarps are made from tissue paper drenched in diluted white glue. When they are rolled and tied with a string they should dry thoroughly prior to painting.

Sidewall detail of the MDA Middle East Ruin kit. Note the very life-like structure of the masonry and plaster.

The remainders of the first floor with a liberal amount of debris. The broken window is a piece of glass from a slide frame.

With a little effort very realistic shutters can be made from plasticard.

The everpresent Coke promotion. The sign was cut from a magazine ad.

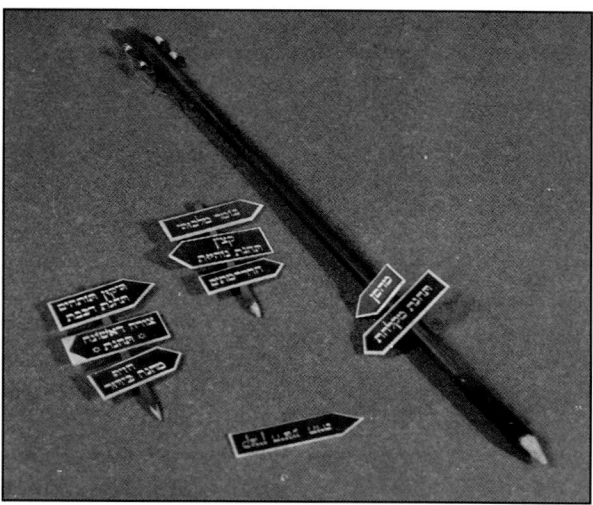

The Italeri telephone pole and custom Hebrew road signs.

A close-up of the tank with a suitable poster as background.

Details on the electronic gun-laying equipment are of course classified, but considered the amount of 'brains' Israel can rely on (many a genious is jewish), the stuff must be state-of-art, which means better than the average western electronic goodies. It is a known fact that Israeli tank crews are amongst the best, if not the best, in the world. Their incredible score in battle is enough evidence.

The Tamiya kit of the Merkava is the result of a new trend to pay some more attention to modern armor. The M-1 Abrams and M-998 Sgt. York are other examples. The model is a delight to build. Detail is hard to believe and very accurate. Just the exhausts need some attention and an external fire extinguisher has to be added. This is due to the fact that Tamiya wanted to keep the mold for the hull top simple, thus cheap. Apart from that it is just a matter of assembling and painting.

The French paratrooper figure from Chota Sahib adds authentic realism to the scene.

Breach to Victory

This little scene depicts an M5 Stuart passing a Siegfried Line roadblock in late fall 1944. The tough fighting at the massive concrete defence system on the German west border finally resulted in some breeches being blown in this West Wall through which the 3rd US Amry could roll into Germany. This marked the beginning of the end for the Third Reich.

The model is the M5 kit from Tamiya with some extra details added, and manned with a crew from converted figures.

The MDA 'Siegfried Line roadblock' kit (MDA 35301) consist of three small dragon theeth, one larger one and a passage blocking construction that can take four I-beams. This sort of anti-tank defence is typical for the West Wall, some good remainders can still be seen along the German border from Switzerland to the Netherlands. They will most likely stay there for ever, since it would cost a fortune to blow them to pieces. The dragon theeth are all interconnected underground. Actually they are nasty pyramids sticking up from one large, continuous concrete slab about three feet thick. It took divisional heavy artillery days to take out a small section, leaving a ploughed up ground with big hunks of concrete, unpassable for armor. In other words, the infantry had to seize the roadblocks at very high cost to open up the Line for the armored forces.

A topview of the M5 turret. As was, and is, so typical for US troops, the vehicle is loaded with equipment. On the turret you can see a map case, documents, a Thompson gun and a steel helmet. The tank commander was put together from parts of Italeri and Tamiya figures. Note the dust goggles, shoulder harness and wiring coming down from the headset.

The engine deck is also piled up with equipment as there are bedrolls and tarps made from tissue paper, kitsacks from epoxy putty, C-rations from VP and jerrycans with fresh water.

The steel I-beams of the roadblock are Plastastruct profiles. The sign and barbed wire are from VP. A nice detail is the waterfilled pudhole with a floating jerrycan and MP 40 sticking out. Also note the German helmet on one of the poles.

The front of the M5 is loaded with sandbags made from epoxy putty for additional protection. The sandbags were placed while the putty was still soft to guarantee a proper sit. Amongst the small details are again a steel helmet, a shovel, military cardboard box from VP and a tow cable made from model ship rope.

The concrete construction that takes the four I-beams which serve as tank obstruction in the dragon theeth defence line. Of course you will find one on both sides of the road.

An overall view of the diorama breathing the atmosphere of late fall 1944. After a beautiful summer it got cold, wet and muddy, not very stimulating for the fighting soldier.

Commander's Delight

Above: A typical Grafenwöhr scene as we have seen it. A unit commander in adoration for 'his guns', displacing to another firing point.

Below: The Tamiya M151 'Ford Mutt' (US soldiers do not know what a Ford Mutt is) with additional detail to make it a typical unit commander's jeep. Note the extra radio sets, maps, helmets with camouflage covers and so on.

In recent years Tamiya initiated the release of modern AFV models with their M1 Abrams and M988 Sgt. York. Rumour has it they are now working on the M2/3 Bradley. The other major producer of military models, Italeri, could not but follow this trend and they released the M108/109 SP Howitzer series. It is a true shame, but Italeri is no longer what it used to be. No longer do they offer the quality that used to be their trademark, on the contrary not only are the latest models very basic, they also often have a load of faults.

In case of the SP howitzer that is subject of this diorama, they denote it as being an M109A2. It is not! You can either make an ML109A1 or A3 straight from the box, but definitely not the A2. To turn the model in the A2 you have to remove the floatation kit equipment from the bow and the hull top. Furthermore the tube is too long and the model in its entirety lacks lots of details.

The diorama shows an M109A2 of 1st Armored DivArty on excersise on the Grafenwöhr range in Germany. The main feature is the VP modern US armor crew, which consists of three beautifully sculpted pewter figures that finally allow you to make a life-like scene.

This picture illustrates how much detail has to be added to make this model a true replica of the M109A2. There were times when you would find all this detail as a standard on Italeri models. You could even take detailing further by removing the integrated hinges of all doors and replace them by seperate ones.

The additional details on the gunmount in detail. Bolts, nuts, covers, boresighting equipment mounts, lots have to be improved. Note the detail around the driver's hatch. Under the turret you can still see the traces of what used to be the cover over the pressure lines of the floatation kit. It was sanded off, a critical operation since it leaves very thin plastic in this area. Note that the barrel was shortened by removing the part of the tube on the gunmount.

Although a lot of detailing is involved, this final result illustrates that the kit is still worthwhile to build. The details that have to be added are not too hard to make, but that does not mean they should not have been there in the first place. The result is however worthwhile the trouble. The vehicle is finished in the MERDC pattern and, as always, loaded with personel equipment. The beautiful armor crew is the finishing touch.

Lots of the action happens of the turret roof. Of course you find all the classic stuff like kitsacks, tarps, bedrolls, staff maps, personel arms, rations and so on and so forth. Noteworthy are the canvas cover over the gunmount made from tissue paper, the smooth weldbeads along the roofplate and the white striping on the gunmount. Also note the very natural pose of the figures.

The painted tankcrew in detail. The masterly sculpting is beyond compare. There is so much authentic detail that painting these beauties is a real joy, that is, unless you hate painting figures. The flesh parts were painted with oil paints on a basecoat of desert sand. The uniforms were painted with Humbrol colors.

Notable details on the diorama include the authentic signs and lost track links.

The unit commander's jeep with trailer. Note the orange flashlight, mandatory on all military vehicles in Germany.

Heavy Weight Centipede

Kit conversion by Eddy JANSSENS

In recent years a series of highly detailed European trucks were released by Italeri. This, plus a visit to Belgian army barracks gave birth to the idea to build a heavy armor transporter on 24th scale. A set of color slides and a brochure of the DAF trailer gave the final go-ahead.

The basis for the tractor is the Italeri MAN 4 x 6 kit (n° 756). The chassis had to be lengthened 25mm to accomodate the pair of home-made heavy duty winches. The original tractor being a 6 x 6, the front axle from the kit had to be replaced by a scratchbuilt drive train. The distributor gearbox was attached to the kit's engine-transmission assembly. The ground clearance of the chassis had to be increased by approx. 5mm.

The cab was lengthened by 7mm. The aft portion was cut off along the aft side windows and 7mm wide heavy plasticard added. Careful filling and sanding rendered the scars of this plastic surgery invisible. New windows were cut from clear styrene.

The Italeri kit features pressed steel rims. They were replaced by six-spoke cast wheels from a Mack DM600 truck (Ertl n° 8018). The wheels of a second same kit were used for the trailer. By good fortune the 25th scale spoke wheels fit exactly in the 24th scale Italeri rims. One does not meet with that sort of luck every day.

As said, the winches were scratchbuilt using detail slides as a guide. To provide for the jerrycans, a few Esci kits of the Camel Trophy Range Rover had to be cannibalised.

The DAF trailer was entirely scratchbuilt from plastic sheet, while styrene I-beams from Faller were used for the front support. The sixteen wheels plus spare hail from the Mack DM600 kit, as said. The many details were constructed from plastic rod and strip and numerous items from the scrapbox. The reflectors are from the Mack kit, while Armtec chains were used on the winches and trailer.

Tractor and trailer were airbrushed with a mixture of two parts US Marines green and one part dark earth to obtain the correct khaki drab shade. A fair coat of matt varnish protects the base color from the wear of the weathering procedure. The various shades of dirt deposits were accomplished by using powdered pastel chalks.

It took a few months of fanatic scratchbuilding, a series of less-civilised words and even more patience before this heavy duty armor transport combination was finished. Now I am constantly being asked by fellow modelers: '..... and what are you going to put on that trailer, a M109A1 SP, a Leopard..... ??!!'

The completely finished heavy armor transporter as it is being used by the Belgian army. Note the width indicators on the tractor's bumper and the swanneck shape of the front part of the trailer.

The MAN tractor with extra equipment as there are: double winches, sheaves for cables, toolbox, racks with jerrycans and a towbar on the rear bumper.

Above: A frontal view of the tractor. The radiator grill from the kit has been replaced by a homemade one of authentic design.
Right: Right side view of the lengthened cab. Note the six-spoke rim in the Italeri wheel.

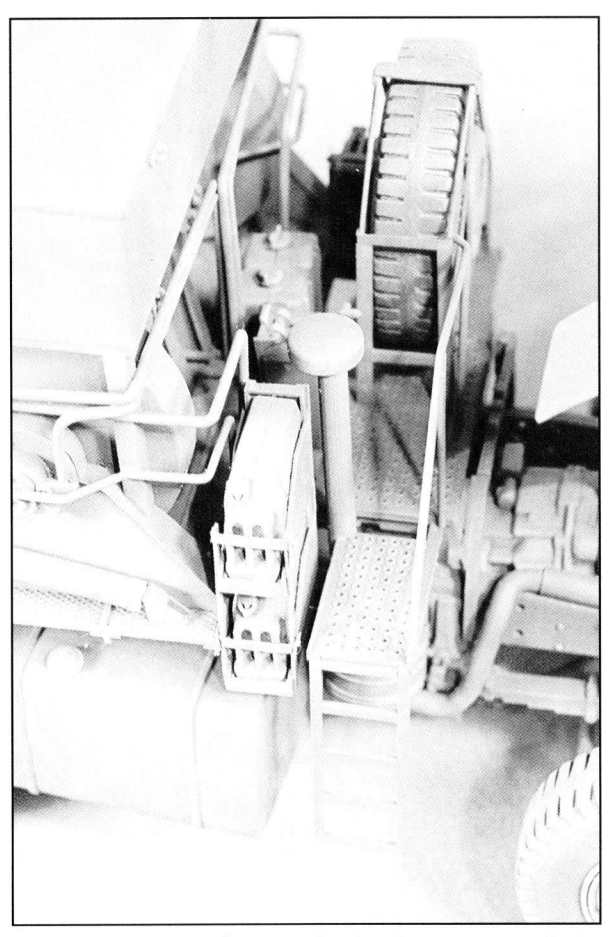

A detail shot of the air intake system, winch controls, jerrycan rack and hydraulic and pneumatic lines for the winches.

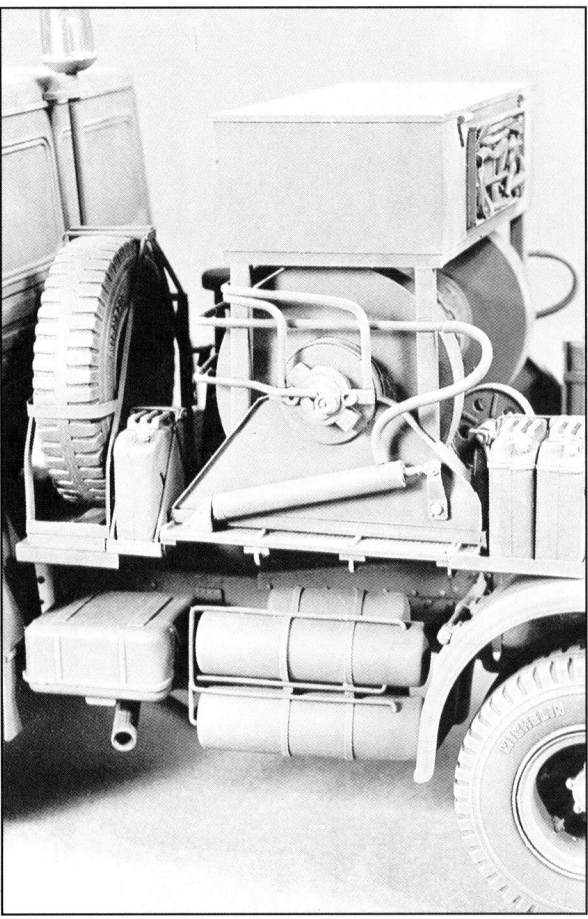

A left side view showing detail of the winches, spare wheel rack, battery case and airpressure cylinders with their lines.

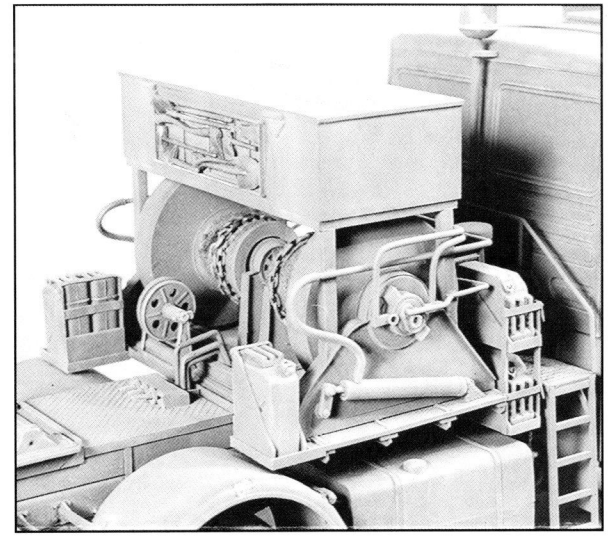

This right quarter view shows how the winches are mounted. Needless to say that you cannot do without plastic rod and strip.

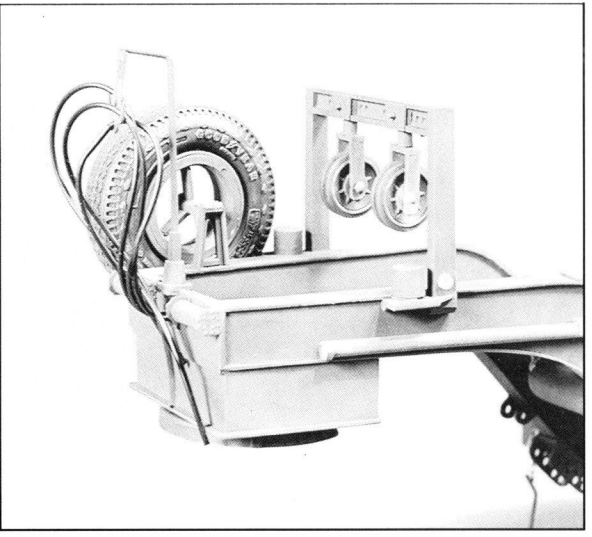

The front section of the trailer features sheaves to guide the steel cables in case a disabled vehicle has to be pulled onto the trailer.

Right hand close-up showing the spare tyre and the adjustable sheave assembly.

The rear section of the trailer. Here the original wheels of the Ertl Mack kit were used.

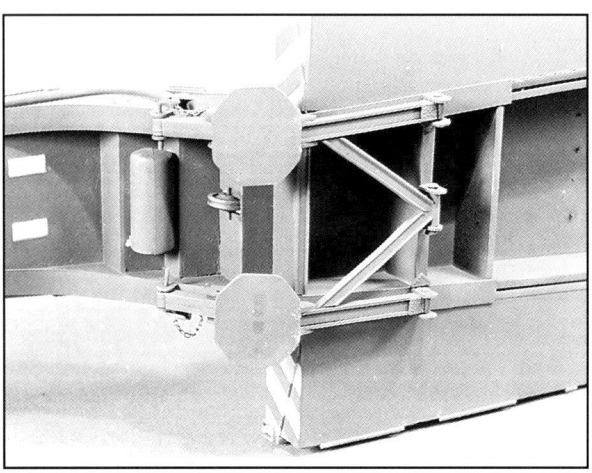

Faller HO beams were used to construct these front supports.

The cargo platform features servicing hatches and anti-skid strips for tracked vehicles.

Imagine getting a flat tyre! It would give you a complex.

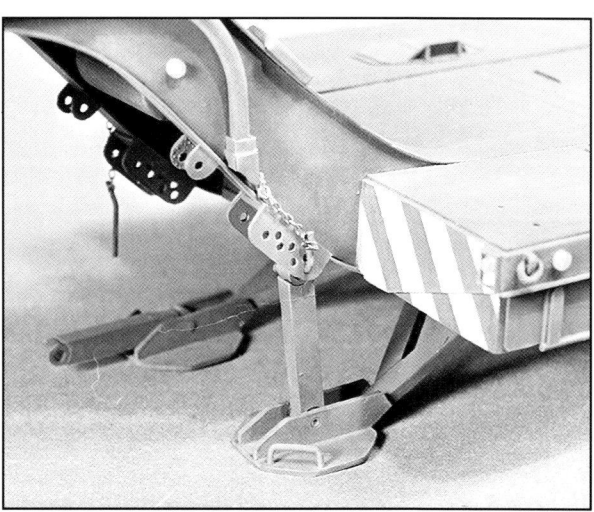

Detail shot of the lowered front support. Note the height adjustment holes.

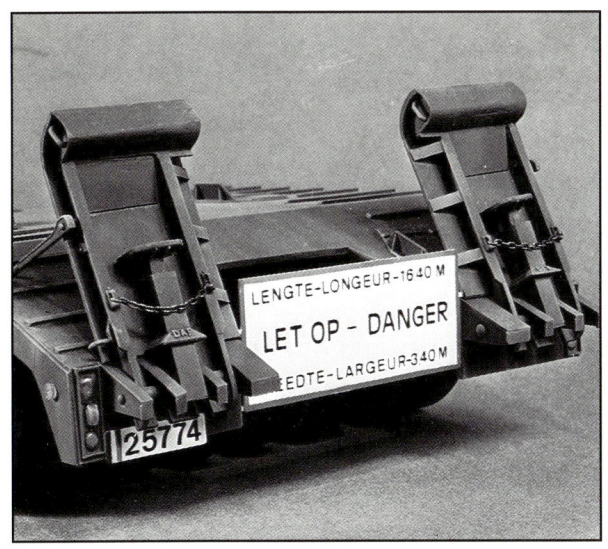

This view shows, in detail, the raised loading ramps with adjustable supports. The warning sign and registration plate are simple pieces of plasticard with dry transfers.

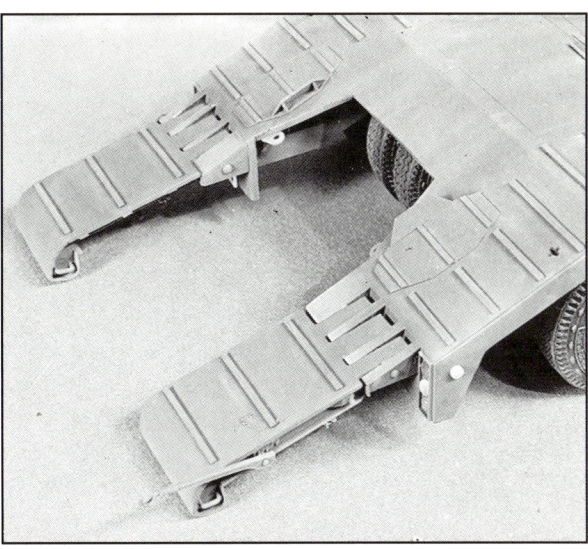

The loading ramps have been lowered. The anti-skid strips offer tracked vehicles some grip on the sloping ramps.

The finished trailer. Of course it has the necessary cable lugs, stowage bins for chains and such, reflectors and hydraulic and electric connections for the brakes and signals.

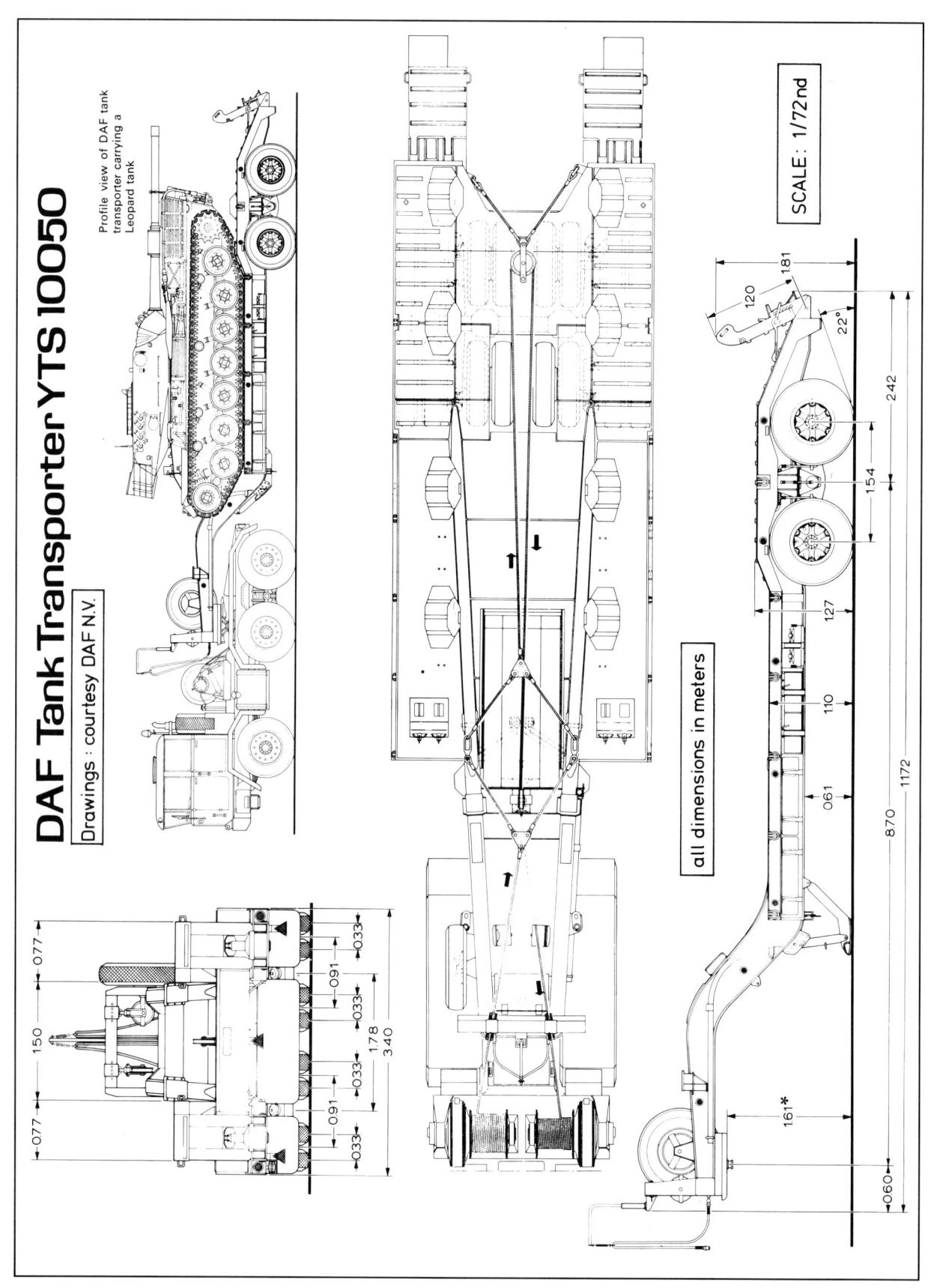

Knocked Out!

This diorama is a challenge for every modeler. It is the result of years of experience. The construction of the kit, the airbrushing of model and accessories, superdetailing and weathering, nothing really went by the book. The entire scene is one large example of improvisation that is based on the knowledge of what can and cannot be done. Moreover, creativity should be written in capitals.

The idea for this diorama has been in my mind for a long time. Over the years I have been figuring out the lay-out of the scene and made up a list of all the items I would need to create a balanced whole. Whenever I thought the time to be right, it turned out that this or that was not available. Although I finally sat down and did it, you still will not find the majority of the accessories in your hobby shop. For instance, there still are no serious figures on the 1/24 scale that has been so popular for decades. Instead, Tamiya has been fooling around on 1/20 and 1/12 scale. There are no seperate tools, hardly any accessories, no spare parts kits and so on. Most of what you see here is home-made, gathered by canabalizing other kits or converted.

The diorama shows a Mini Cooper S rally car being serviced and repaired after a competition. The magnificent 24th scale model is from Tamiya, who have recently started a range of classic cars. Since I needed spare parts to make a realistic scene, I used two kits.

The figure is from Tamiya's 'Campus Friends' set, the tools were taken from their 1/20 scale tool set, some VP accessories were used, all the rest was scratchbuilt or converted.

On the next five pages you will find an illustrated, step-by-step description of how this diorama came to be.

I started by constructing and finishing the car model. Should this fail to come out right, the rest would be a waste of time, if already finished. All casting seams and flash were removed with sanding paper and steel wool. The decals were applied directly to the plastic and the whole was coated with semi-gloss varnish. This picture illustrates the initial stages of weathering.

A rear quarter view of the finished model. Heavy weathering is quite in place on a rally car. The dust and dried mud was airbrushed on and blended with the body color with fine steel wool. Note the straps that secure the spare wheels on the rack.

Front quarter view of the finished mean Mini. The shattered windshield was simulated by cutting the original clear part to pieces. The cracks were scribed with a needle. The pieces were then fixed with white glue.

The finished engine is installed in the chassis. The ignition cables and fuel and oil lines are made from copper wire in several gages. Painting and weathering the engine was mainly guesswork since I only had the kit instructions to go by. Note the chipped paint on the air filter cover.

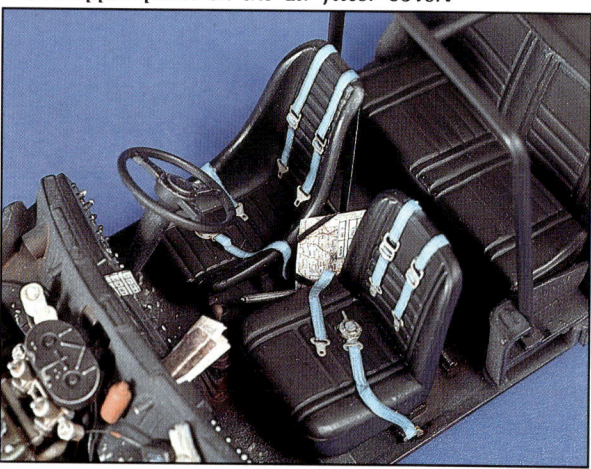

Main feature in the finished interior are the safety harnesses. The buckles are VP 24th scale race car buckles while the straps are made of graphic tape. The roadmaps tugged between the seats and in the dashboard are also from VP.

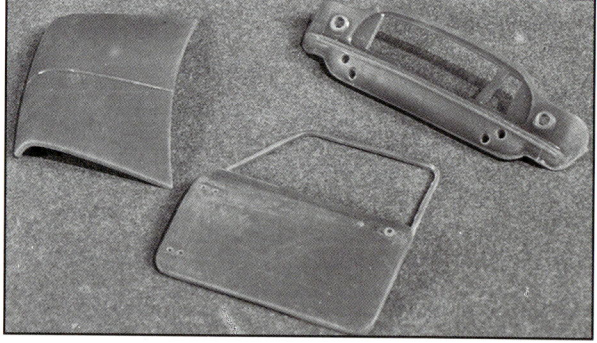

The body spare parts are ready for painting. They were carefully cut from the second model, filed and sanded. The hinges were cut off and bolt holes drilled.

The spare parts rack in the workshop was home-made using 3mm square rod from Tamiya and plastic sheet.

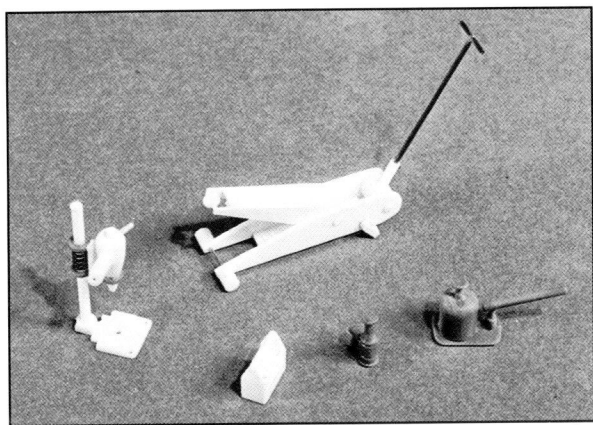

The home-made tabletop drill stand was made using some rod and sheet, a spring and a hydraulic wrench from the Tamiya pit set. The rolling hydraulic jack is entirely scratchbuilt.

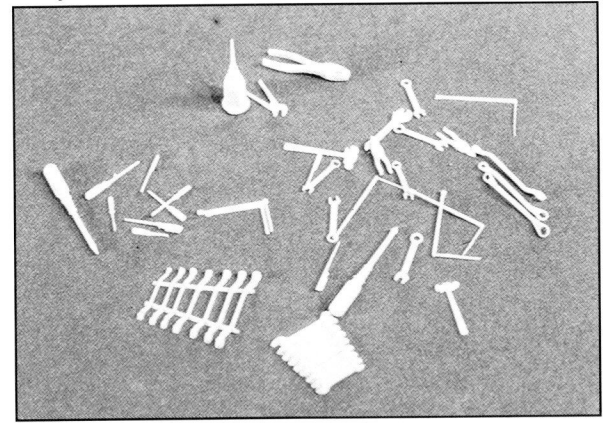

A large array of tools. The majority was carefully sanded off the back of the toolbox that comes with the Tamiya 1/20 scale racing pit set.

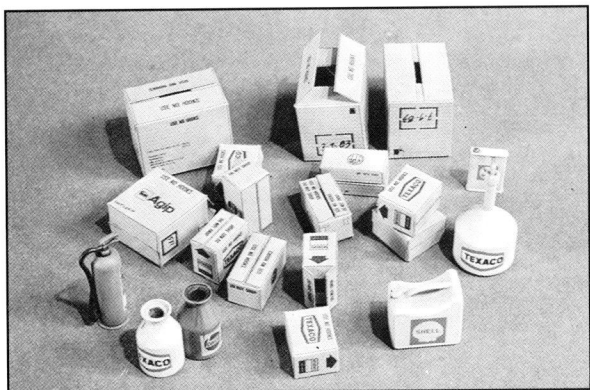

The assortment of cardboard boxes are again from VP. You can assemble them either opened or closed. The oil cans and fire extinguisher were taken from the Tamiya 1/20 scale racing pit set.

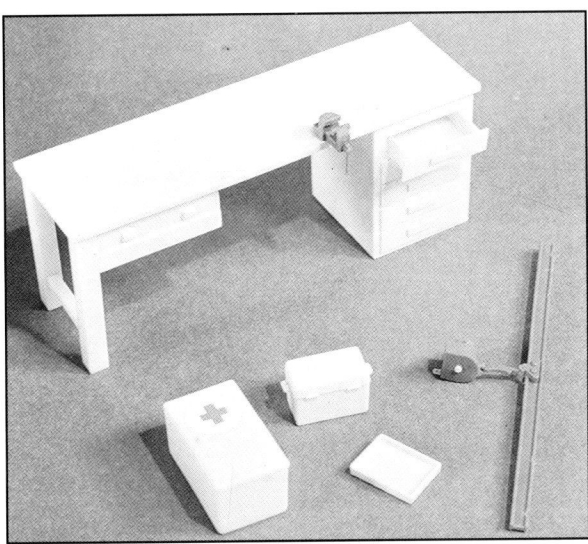

The workbench consists of plastic sheet and square rod. The first aid kit, coolbox and oil pan were taken from the Tamiya set. The I-beam with hoist was not used on the diorama since I skipped the original idea of adding a ceiling.

A first test lay-out of the diorama to figure out the best position of the major components and establish the dimensions of the baseplate.

The floor and walls of the workshop are finished. The walls were made from fine styrofoam sheet. The I-beams between the sections are Plastastruct items. The floor is a simple piece of cardboard airbrushed in dark red and weathered with pastels and thinned black paint as oil stains.

A simple electric installation was made from plastic rod and strip. The fluorescent lamps are 1mm rod from Tamiya. The steel door is again made from sheet and strip.

The rack is stuffed with spare parts that mostly come from the second mini Cooper kit and of course the well-known scrapbox. The cardboard boxes add that extra touch of realism.

A messy workbench so typical for most workshops. The spare engine is under repair. Note the various small touches of realism as there are the empty beer bottles, oily rags, scattered tools and beverage cans on the bench as well as the first aid kit and box under it. When all items are fixed in place, they are weathered with pastels and thinned black paint.

The Mini is jacked up at one side for some underside repair. Note the scattered tools on the fender and the floor. The inspection lamp was made from leftovers, while soldering wire is used for the power line.

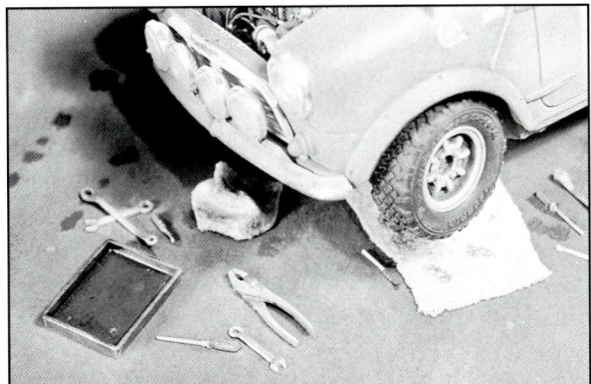

The tool for the mechanic effecting the underside repair are close at hand. Since there is no lying mechanic on 24th scale, we assume he went out to the restroom for a minute. Note the oil pan with wasted oil. This is simply dirty black paint with a heavy coat of gloss varnish on top of it.

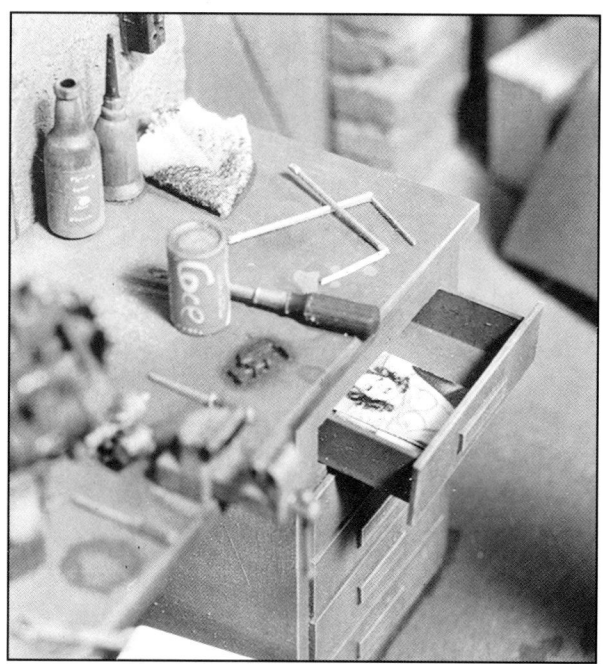

The right part of the workbench shows some of the tools, coke cans and beer bottles in detail. Noticed the mechanics favourite pass-time in the drawer?

A closer look at the rack shows the details on the cardboard boxes and the centerfolds on the wall.

The table-top drill stand is on the left side of the bench. Again the power line is soldering wire.

The spare parts were airbrushed in light grey and dusted with pastels. A fake code number was added in thinned white paint.

VERLINDEN PRODUCTIONS

VERLINDEN & STOK pvba
BERLAARSESTRAAT 36
2500 LIER · BELGIUM

offers you everything to turn your dioramas into **MASTERPIECES**

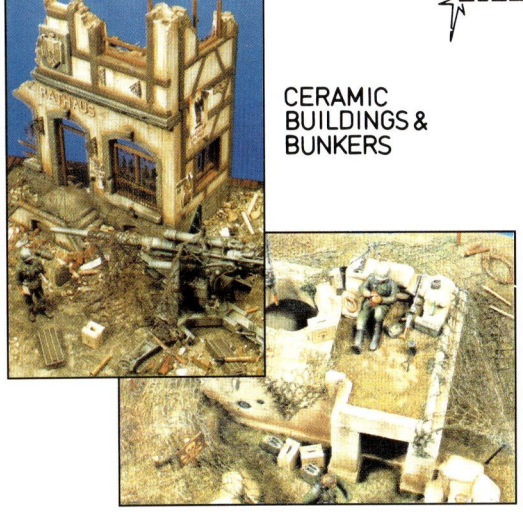

CERAMIC BUILDINGS & BUNKERS

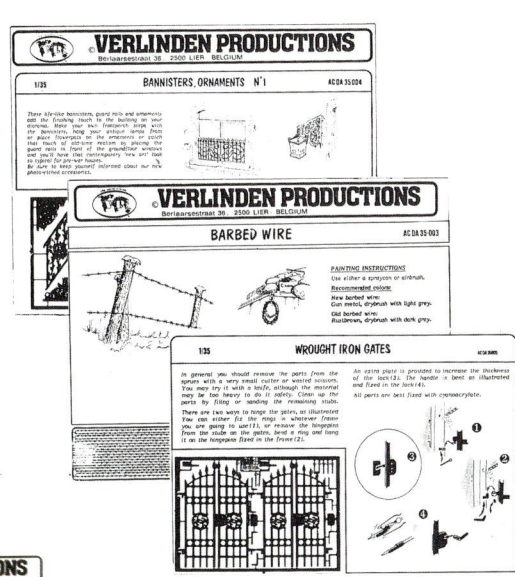

PHOTO-ETCHED PARTS

FULL COLOR 35th SCALE COMMERCIAL SIGNS & ROAD SIGNS

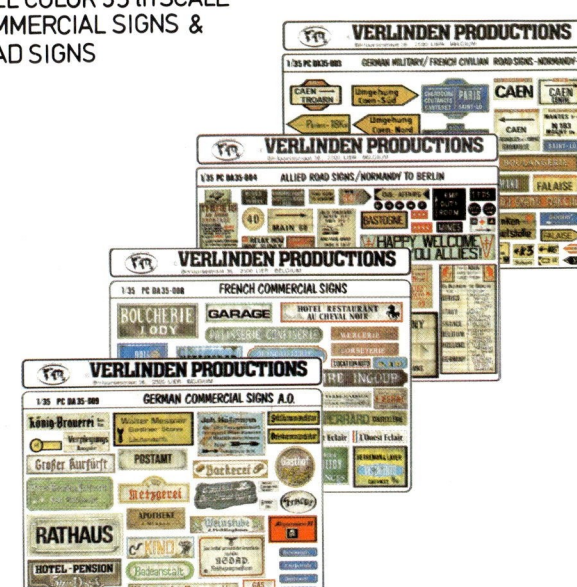

FULL COLOR 35th SCALE POSTERS

VERLINDEN PRODUCTIONS

VERLINDEN & STOK pvba
BERLAARSESTRAAT 36
2500 LIER - BELGIUM

THE LIFE-LIKE FINISHING TOUCH FOR YOUR MILITARY MODELS

54mm FIGURES
U.S. & ISRAELI TANK CREW

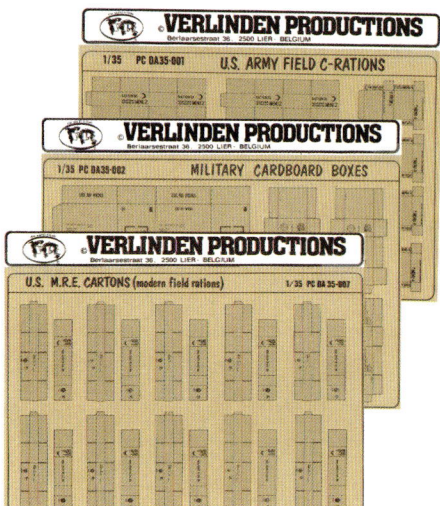

PREPRINTED CARTON BOXES

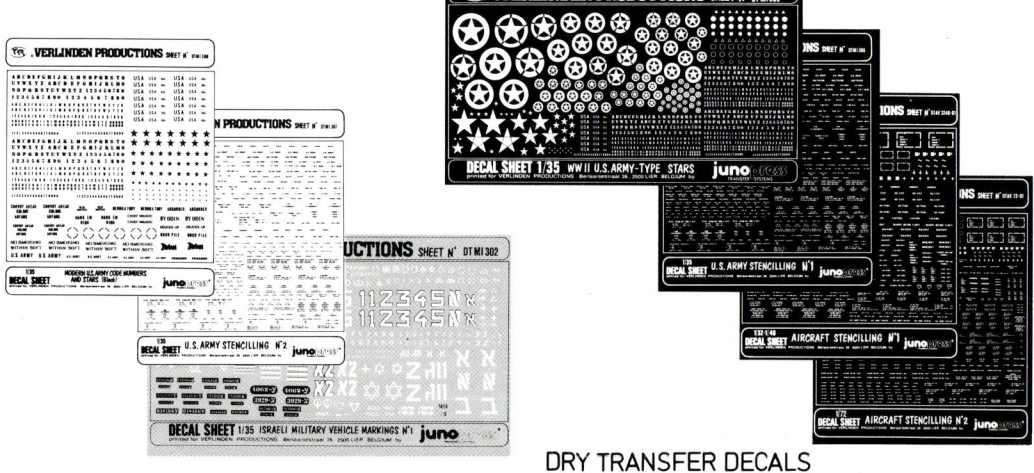

DRY TRANSFER DECALS